OUR YEAR

EUROPEAN CHAMPIONS 2022

OUR YEAR

EUROPEAN CHAMPIONS 2022

Reach Sport
www.reachsport.com

Published in Great Britain and Ireland in 2022 by
Reach Sport, a Reach PLC business,
5 St Paul's Square, Liverpool, L3 9SJ.

www.reachsport.com
@Reach_Sport

Reach Sport is a part of Reach PLC.
One Canada Square, Canary Wharf, London, E15 5AP.

Production Editor: Roy Gilfoyle
Executive Art Editor: Rick Cooke
Words: Alice McKeegan, Aidan McCartney, Mat Kendrick, Matt Smith, Oscar Haley, Shane Ireland, Peter Staunton, Chris Brereton
Design: Chris Collins, Adam Ward, Mark Frances, Neil Haines

ISBN: 9781914197666

Photographic acknowledgements:
Getty Images, Alamy

Printed and bound by Bell & Bain.

Reach Sport
www.reachsport.com

LONDON
UEFA WOMEN'S EURO ENGLAND 2022
LONDON
INNERS + + WIN
+ + WINNERS + + WINNERS
CRAWLEY
POLICE
POLICE
POLICE

CONTENTS

FOREWORD

CHASE YOUR DREAMS

BY SARINA WIEGMAN

This is more than a football story.

Over the pages of this book, fans will be able to relive the happiness and excitement of England's EURO 2022 triumph.

You will be able to read about the journey of a grounded group who worked so hard to deliver that historic moment on Sunday, July 31.

But ours is a success story which is about more than just sport.

There will be lots of girls and boys so inspired by our summer win that they too will dream of putting on their boots to score a winner at Wembley like Chloe Kelly.

We certainly hope so because we have been touched by the support we have received from the entire nation and we want to keep the momentum rolling for as long as possible.

However, what we achieved and the way we went about it should hopefully live with non-football fans as well.

Our story – a real life fairytale – is as much about life lessons than the football on the pitch.

This is about who you are, who you want to be, where you want to go and how you intend on getting there.

I'm often asked what message I have for children and my answer is simple; chase your dreams.

Do what you love the most and just go for it. If you want to do it, do it and don't let anybody tell you otherwise.

If you want to follow our players and lift the European Championship trophy, that's great.

But what we as a team want to show more than anything is that whatever you decide to be just be the best version of yourselves.

It's very hard to describe how incredibly proud I am of this team and the togetherness of this group.

There is one thing the players did after the Euros triumph that makes me burst with pride more than anything else. It's the powerful letter they sent to the Government to protect and honour our legacy by ensuring schoolgirls have equal access to football.

Our players didn't start playing football because they wanted to make history and have a voice, they just love the game.

I didn't start coaching because I wanted to make history and have a voice, I just love the game.

Now we're not only making history but we have a platform to make a difference and that is a wonderful outcome of being successful.

It means we must continue to be our best, show respect and use this moment in women's football to affect positive change.

I'll borrow a phrase from that brilliant open letter to sign off: 'We see this as only the beginning...'

Enjoy the book and while we're trying to write our next chapter, have fun writing yours.

euro
ENGLAND 2022

ENGLAND 2022
ENGLAND 2022
ENGLAND V GERMANY
31 JULY 2022
UEFA WOMENS EURO FINAL
CAP

OUR CAPTAIN

A SMILE TO LIGHT UP WEMBLEY

Williamson's inspirational story the perfect example of how to 'be yourself'

BY MAT KENDRICK

Let's start with the gumshield story.

A missing mouth protector might seem like a strange way to kick off a glowing tribute to the first England football captain to lift a major trophy since the late, great Bobby Moore, but the gumshield story provides an intriguing introduction into the making of Leah Williamson.

Growing up in a sports-mad family in Milton Keynes in the early noughties, Williamson tried her hand at swimming and gymnastics before the thrilling realisation she had the world at her feet.

Mum, Amanda, herself a keen footballer who had her own hair cut short to fit in with the boys in her youth, encouraged her only daughter to try out with local lads' team, Scot's Youth FC. That was on the condition that little Leah protected with a gumshield a smile that would ultimately go on to light up Wembley, the Emirates Stadium and the regular home of Arsenal Women, Meadow Park.

Amanda even got a mouthguard with a St George's flag on to please her England-mad six-year-old as the future national team captain bravely took her first steps in a game she would, to the surprise and delight of the tight-knit Williamsons and eventually the entire country, completely excel at.

Grandma Bernie had other ideas about the gumshield. When nan rather than mum

was the matchday chauffeur, Williamson would lay it on thick, complaining that she couldn't breathe properly with the shield in place. This prompted Bernie to disobey Amanda's firm instructions and let Leah decide for herself how to look after her teeth and herself on the football field.

"She's a bad influence!" joked Amanda, finally learning of her daughter and mother's good-natured deceit on a sentimental return visit to Scot's Youth FC many years later.

On the contrary. At a time when Williamson has become football's ultimate influencer thanks to the example she sets to girls and young women, it is crucial to recognise the part her own role models played.

Family is everything to Williamson and if you ever wondered how a strong, independent future England women's football captain was created back then look no further than Amanda and Bernie for your answer.

It is not just the female influence, though. To this day, her pre-match superstition is to carry in her kitbag poems her dad David wrote for her and his supportive role in her meteoric rise is not to be underestimated, likewise her strong bond with her brother Jacob.

Protecting by empowering is a common theme throughout the England skipper's development and is in keeping with the way Sarina Wiegman has engineered an elite mentality throughout her squad, with Williamson as a young, but natural leader.

While her mum backed her to beat the boys despite the stigma of being the only girl, and her nan trusted her to make her own safety decisions despite the risks, Williamson's male teammates at Scot's Youth FC looked after her by treating her as one of their own.

Tackling her with as much force in training as they would each other, so that when she was kicked for real in competitive matches, it didn't ruffle her. She knew full well that overcoming opponents with her ability was the perfect riposte.

It is a grounding that continues to serve her and the national team well.

Despite starring for the boys' team at 'my little Wembley', the Scots Sport and Social Club in Bletchley, Williamson's footballing ambitions might have been for the high jump – or rather the long jump – because of the previous big spectacle on home soil to truly ignite the nation's sporting flame, the 2012 Olympics.

Williamson's home of Milton Keynes is also known for long jumper Greg Rutherford, whose great strides and golden leap a decade ago inspired so many, including the city's most famous daughter, to strive for national prominence.

Fleetingly she considered ditching football to follow Rutherford into athletics. By then she had already followed Dean McBroom, her youth team mentor at Rushden and Diamonds, to Arsenal, but Rutherford's gold medal heroics did convince her that

'GOING FROM FANGIRL WITH A PHOTO OF [KELLY] SMITH ON HER BEDROOM WALL TO PARADING THE FA CUP AROUND WEMBLEY WITH HER ICON WAS JUST ONE OF A RECURRING THEME OF 'PINCH YOURSELF' MOMENTS'

ordinary boys and girls from a modest corner of Buckinghamshire really could dream big.

Aged nine, when she was snapped up by Arsenal's academy, Williamson fully immersed herself in football and the rest, as they say, is genuine football history.

Raised by a family with its own north London divide – half Spurs, half Arsenal – Williamson was always a Gunner, idolising Thierry Henry and progressing to an adulation for women's legend Kelly Smith, which was to bring its own challenges.

Going from fangirl with an autographed photo of Smith on her bedroom wall to parading the FA Cup around Wembley with her childhood icon was just one of a recurring series of 'pinch yourself' moments she greeted with a very grounded gratitude.

Getting a glimpse into the future as a League Cup mascot for the men's team away at West Bromwich Albion in 2006 and as a Champions League final mascot for Arsenal Women during their finest hour in 2007 were goose-bump dress rehearsals that served to inspire rather than intimidate her.

In fact, since her Gunners debut as a 17-year-old substitute in a 2-0 European defeat to Birmingham City in 2014, alongside the stars she grew up worshipping, she has never been anything other than a consummate team player, comfortable in her own skin and with an empathy and emotional intelligence that have indelibly etched her into football folklore by her mid-twenties.

Once she made it into the senior side, those initial starstruck moments were quickly replaced by a desire to establish herself as a first-team regular and a winning one at that.

She has barely been on the planet a quarter of a century, yet she already boasts a Women's Super League title, two FA Cups and two League Cups – and that is before even mentioning a creaking trophy cabinet full of individual honours and her international successes.

Before jubilantly raising that shiny much-coveted EURO trophy above her head on

a balmy summer's day at Wembley on Sunday, July 31, Williamson always ranked her England debut as the most special highlight in a career already packed full of them.

It came as an 84th-minute replacement for close pal Keira Walsh in a 3-1 World Cup qualifying win over Russia in 2018 and not even the frustration of her usually ever-present family missing that match in Moscow could detract from the satisfaction she felt.

Her relatives were also absent when she did eventually follow Rutherford's Olympics example, representing Great Britain in the Covid-delayed 2020 behind-closed-doors Games in 2021, as the Tokyo adventure ended with a frustrating quarter-final defeat to Australia.

Since then the Williamson clan have more than made up for it – "family is the most important thing in the world," she says – and they were already partying on the streets of Milton Keynes when she officially landed the England captaincy ahead of this summer's Euros, long before the team actually brought the trophy home.

A temperament that belies her relatively young age allowed her to quickly process the privilege of captaining her country: to fully appreciate it, but to cast aside any vulnerabilities by embracing what England needed from her, not the other way round.

It came as no surprise that Williamson took to representing and leading the Lionesses with such poise.

Her football development included a rise through the England age groups and featured a stressful experience that would unnerve hardened veterans, never mind a teenage rookie.

Back in April 2015, Williamson was made to wait FIVE days to retake a crucial penalty with the nation's place at the Under-19s Euro at stake.

It was an unprecedented period of fretting for Williamson after UEFA ruled that she should get a second crack at her spot-kick in the qualifier against Norway.

The initial effort in the original match had been disallowed for encroachment and rather than ordering a retake there and then the referee wrongly awarded a free-kick to the opposition.

Bizarrely, the remaining seconds of the match were replayed on another evening, leaving Williamson to walk straight from the tunnel to the penalty spot at 9.45pm to take the vital kick.

True to form our heroine kept her focus, blocked out any external pressures and did what she does best, delivered for her team in a big moment.

"I would not wish that situation on my worst enemy," she would later admit. "What I went through in those five days was not a normal amount of stress really.

"I was having conversations with the girls 'Tell me she's not going to save it' and they were like 'You know she's not going to save it!'

"I literally thought to myself, why Leah, why do you put yourself in these situations? But it all worked out in the end."

With Williamson it tends to. Such focus and clarity made her Wiegman's ideal go-to girl for the historic, game-changing Euros triumph.

A self-deprecating wit, a knack of leading by example, clear and confident communication skills and the inherent ability to put the team's needs before her personal wants earned her the armband.

She is blessed with an everywoman quality that defines the England squad. Williamson loves a challenge and a cross-field ping and her personal stats saw her make more ball recoveries than any other player during the tournament. Yet her dressing room influence runs much deeper than what she can do with a football.

Her sheer desire for individual and collective excellence enabled her to help implement the head coach's winning mentality into a squad whose unquestionable talent was finally backed up by an unwavering belief they could go all the way.

"I think England have hosted an incredible tournament and we've changed the game in this

ENGLAND 2022
ENGLAND V GERMANY
31 JULY 2022
EFA WOMENS EURO FINAL

'AT A TIME WHEN GIRLS, WOMEN AND YOUNG PEOPLE ARE UNDER PRESSURE TO BE SO MANY THINGS, WILLIAMSON IS SPORT'S PERFECT POSTER GIRL FOR THE 'BE YOURSELF' MESSAGE'

country and hopefully across Europe and across the world," beamed Williamson after England beat Germany 2-1 in the final at Wembley.

"We said we wanted to make our legacy about winning and that's what we did.

"The legacy of the tournament was already made before that final game – what we've done for women and young girls who can look up and aspire to be us."

Why wouldn't girls want to be like Leah Williamson?

Whether she is doing charitable work with Arsenal's Willow Foundation for seriously ill adults, listening to country music, experimenting with bold fashion choices, or enjoying a pre-match ham sandwich, she owns every one of her life choices.

At a time when girls, women and young people in general are under such pressure to be so many things, Williamson is sport's perfect poster girl for the 'be yourself' message.

Among her impressive football highlights reels and her engaging social media posts are impassioned opinions on how society as a whole can learn from the England team and women's football in general.

"I have a problem because we bring children up with this mentality that things have to be segregated and you can't just move freely between whatever you want to do," she declares.

"That just sparks something in me. We still have this situation where we have to put everyone in a box and I don't really understand why.

"If someone has a talent or an interest in something, why do we have to keep them out just because they don't look like the people that are doing it?

"I live my life so unapologetically that I don't really think I fit into a box. I don't fit into a box of what I wear, I don't fit into a box of how I act, especially not how I talk.

"I'm getting uncomfortable with how long it's taking us to figure out that we should just let people be who they want to be.

"Sexuality, gender, religion – there's nothing that you could say in a women's changing room that would shock anyone. That's what I love about it.

"But you go into society and it's a different story still."

No wonder Williamson's loving mum was so keen to protect her daughter's mouth all those years ago – not only does our captain have glittering footsteps to follow in, it is all backed up by a powerful voice that simply must not be ignored.

ENGLAND V
31 JULY
UEFA WOMENS
8

OUR LEADER

SARINA WIEGMAN

BY PETER STAUNTON

"We've changed society," Sarina Wiegman said after England won the European Championship title.

And it was hard to argue.

England's victory – on home soil at Wembley against Germany – was a watershed moment not only for football but for sport overall, for women and girls and truly, in the words of head coach Wiegman, for society.

The tournament success brought England's first senior football title since the men's team claimed the World Cup in 1966 and its impact has been seismic.

Messages of congratulations flowed from the world of sport, from politics, from entertainment and from Her Majesty Queen Elizabeth II.

Women and girls have been inspired to get out and play, no matter their level, and the country emboldened to believe anything is possible.

For too long it felt like winning a senior tournament was an insurmountable block for an England team, but this band of Lionesses put that theory to bed once and for all.

It was a breakthrough, a significant milestone, a culmination of a sensational summer which made England believe in itself.

From the moment England beat one of the tournament favourites Norway 8-0 in their second group-stage game – a competition record scoreline – the touchpaper was lit.

Wiegman had to miss the 5-0 final group-stage victory against Northern Ireland due to illness but the best was yet to come when she returned to her place on the bench for the knock-outs.

The dramatic extra-time victory over Spain was a tantalising hint that England were

+ WINNERS +
+ WINNERS +
+ WINNERS +
+ WINNERS +
LONDON
JOIN US
HUBLOT
VISA
VISA
pepsi MAX
TikTok
UEFA WOMEN'S EURO 2022

gathering an unstoppable momentum, that fate would be with them and they had the mental fortitude to overcome difficult situations.

Sweden were seen off comprehensively in the semi-finals after what had been an initially cagey affair; Alessia Russo gave the nation its most iconic moment of the tournament – an impudent backheel for the third and crucial goal, and one which was watched millions of times across television and social media.

The final against Germany at Wembley was a historic occasion, in front of 87,192 people. That figure is now a European Championship record in both the men's and women's game.

The final itself was a cagey encounter but its impact will be felt across English sport and society forevermore. Chloe Kelly's landmark extra-time goal – and subsequent celebration – was more than enough to inspire the record audience at Wembley and the millions more watching at home and in pubs and clubs up and down the country.

England had done it; they had changed society.

At the heart of it all was a thorough and driven woman.

Sarina Wiegman is one of the greatest head coaches in the women's game today. Steeped in the history of the sport, having witnessed first-hand the explosion of women's football in the United States alongside some of that nation's early football legends, her work with her native country – the Netherlands – was extraordinary and set that country on the path for European and – very nearly – global dominance.

And now her work with England too – inspiring a generation – will be remembered forever.

TOWARDS HIGHER STANDARDS

A fiercely competitive midfielder during her playing days, Wiegman was first drafted into the Netherlands international set-up aged only 16.

She made her debut for the national team against Norway under the one and only Dick Advocaat, who took charge of the women's side for a solitary game in 1987.

Wiegman would go on to make 104 appearances in Dutch orange, although only 99 of those caps would ultimately count towards her official total.

A major milestone in her career came after attending the very first, yet still unofficial, women's "World Cup" in China in 1988, where Anson Dorrance, the United States manager, invited her to study and play at the University of North Carolina.

She took up that offer, starring alongside burgeoning USWNT legend Mia Hamm, and would go on to win the 1989 Women's College Cup with the all-conquering Tar Heels.

That achievement she once described as the highlight of her playing career. And, moreover, it opened her eyes to the standards being set in the women's game in the US.

"Abroad, there is a different top-sports climate than in our country," she told

AmsterdamFM in 2016. "It was common there that we trained several times a day, every day. You had guidance on all fronts and the level of football was a lot higher. Higher demands were made."

Wiegman returned home to the Netherlands and took up a post teaching PE away from the kind of limelight she'd experienced in the States. She played for Sassenheim-based club Ter Leede for the rest of her career.

Wiegman played on after the birth of her first child but knew it was time to give up after having her second in 2003. From there, her professional destiny was set towards becoming a world-class coach.

It was at Ter Leede where she began her managerial journey, in 2006, winning a league and cup double the following year.

She moved on to ADO Den Haag, where she would win those same two trophies in 2012 and the cup again in 2013.

It was at that point that she moved into the international realm.

BECOMING MUCH BOLDER

Accepting a job with the Dutch football association (KNVB) as an assistant coach for the women's national team, Wiegman was also given responsibility for the coordination of the under-19 national side.

She began her studies for the UEFA Pro Licence in 2015 alongside the likes of men's international team players Bert Kontermann and Roy Makaay, graduating a year later as only the third Dutchwoman to achieve the coaching award.

"A man usually throws himself into a trainer course without a doubt, while a woman always first wonders if she can do it and then thinks about it for a while," she told the KNVB about her studies. "We all have to become much bolder."

Wiegman would go on to make history by becoming the first woman to sit on the bench as coach of a men's professional team. She had served her internship, as part of her licence, at Jong Sparta Rotterdam and was later invited back by the club to replace another coach, Leen van Steensel, who had been hospitalised.

By that time, she'd had her first taste of coaching the senior women's national team, stepping into the breach to lead the side on an interim basis when Roger Reijnders was sacked. Once Arjan van der Laan was confirmed on a permanent basis – in October 2015 – she reverted to her assistant role.

Reijnders had been in charge for the 2015 Women's World Cup campaign, at which the Netherlands made their official tournament debut having featured at the invitational tournament in China in 1988. They underperformed in that competition, however, winning only one group-stage match before elimination in the first knock-out round against Japan.

It was expected that Van der Laan would be in charge for the 2017 European

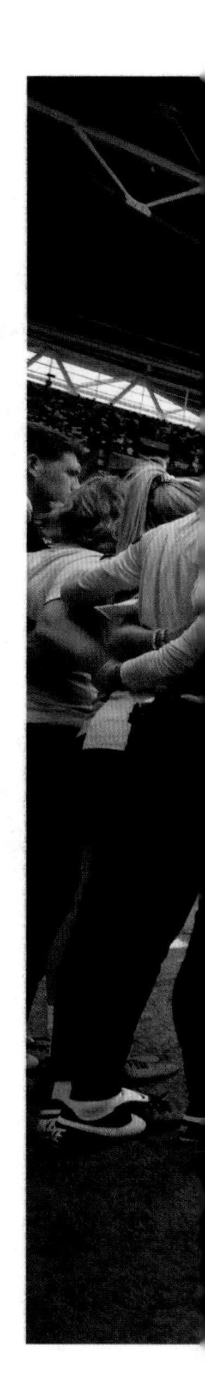

"A MAN USUALLY THROWS HIMSELF INTO A TRAINER COURSE WITHOUT A DOUBT WHILE A WOMAN FIRST WONDERS IF SHE CAN DO IT. WE HAVE TO BECOME MUCH BOLDER"

Top of her game: Sarina Wiegman's path to becoming head coach of England went via the Netherlands and the USA

Championship – on home soil – but he was dismissed in December 2016 with the Dutch side in disarray. A failure to qualify for the 2016 Olympics and four friendly losses out of five cost Van der Laan his job with the association having insufficient confidence in him to provide a solid platform for the European Championship.

And after initially stepping up as an interim coach, it was decided to give Wiegman the job on a permanent basis in January 2017. She signed a contract which would run until after the 2019 World Cup. Her time had truly come.

Playing attacking football, with an emphasis on creativity, the Dutch claimed EURO 2017 with a stunning 4-2 win against Denmark in the final.

They had won three out of three in the group stage – against Norway, eventual finalists Denmark and Belgium – and then stunned Sweden in the quarter-finals. They came up against England, of all teams, in the semis and they convincingly won through, 3-0, in Enschede.

Then, against the Danes, history was made.

As would be later showcased with England, Wiegman put great importance on teamwork and the collective good, best exemplified when Mandy van den Berg – the on-field captain who lost her place in the starting XI during the tournament – hoisted the trophy together with Sherida Spitse in the post-game celebrations.

The tournament win was the high point in the development of women's football in the Netherlands. Commemorative coins were minted and the prime minister Mark Rutte visited the squad in the dressing room after the game.

They had – like England would do five years later – captured the hearts and minds of the public at large with the likes of Lieke Martens and Vivianne Miedema becoming household names to rival anything the men's team could produce.

Vital to that success were Wiegman's principles – asking the squad, for example, in one team meeting, to describe creatively what success would mean to them. In another, it was reported that she distributed an article which listed 13 things you must give up if you are to succeed. Making excuses and wanting to be liked were two of them.

Wiegman's success was all done on a stringent budget too with one estimate putting the Euro-per-player total in the entirety of Dutch women's football at less than €30 per registered member.

But she nonetheless put the Dutch among the elite of the women's game, deservedly claiming her first of two FIFA Women's Coach of the Year awards in 2017.

Although qualification for the 2019 World Cup was a topsy-turvy affair, the Dutch nonetheless managed to make it all the way to the final at only the second time of asking.

The team won three straight group-stage games to qualify in first place ahead of much-fancied Canada.

A thrilling 2-1 victory over Japan followed before a more routine 2-0 win against Italy in the quarter-finals. A solitary extra-time goal in the semis against Sweden set up a final showdown in Lyon against the USWNT.

Hampered by an injury to star Martens, they went down 2-0 to the reigning world champions.

But Wiegman's legacy was secure. Before her tenure, the Dutch team had been bit-part players on the world stage. Under her reign, they hit the big-time; a women's football team to rival anything the world had to offer.

NEW DEPARTURE

England, after an impressive World Cup campaign which featured an inspiring run of their own to the semi-finals, were expected to kick on and mix it consistently among the elite.

Great strides were being made across the country, with efforts from The FA securing a full-time professional league with international players slotting in seamlessly alongside superstar overseas counterparts at club level.

However, things were not going according to plan post-tournament for England on the pitch under their coach Phil Neville, who announced in April 2020 that he would not be renewing his contract, and Wiegman was identified as the first choice to take over. In August 2020, she gave her word to The FA that she would take over from Neville following the Tokyo Olympics.

The Olympics had not gone as hoped for the Dutch, eliminated on penalties at the hands of the USA in the quarter-finals, but her reign had been deemed an immense success with the team rising as high as third in the world rankings.

"What we did with the Dutch national team – and people who were connected to

TOUCHING HANDS...

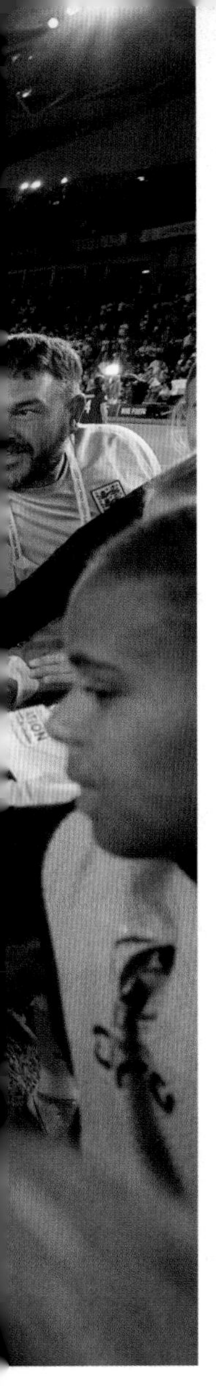

Dutch women's football for a long time laid the foundations, and I continued that together with my colleagues and players – that was a great journey with the EURO, the [FIFA Women's] World Cup final and the Olympic Games," Wiegman said ahead of UEFA Women's EURO 2022.

She would have to hit the ground running. EURO 2022 was fast approaching. England needed a reboot, a way to tap into their unique individual talent and strengthen their collective identity.

First, there was the small matter of 2023 World Cup qualification. Wiegman's first match in charge in that competition ended in an 8-0 win against North Macedonia. At the end of England's autumn / winter qualification campaign, Latvia were clinically beaten by a record scoreline, an astonishing 20-0. Wiegman's record as the year turned was: Played 6, Won 6, Goals For 53, Goals Against 0.

More success was to follow in the 2022 Arnold Clark Cup. World class opposition in the shape of Canada, Spain and Germany faced England. Two draws – against the Canadians and Spain – preceded a 'winner takes all' match for the title against Germany. In a sign of things to come, the spoils went to England as they won 3-1.

England, then, were in terrific shape heading into EURO 2022. They were named among the experts' favourites, even if the country as yet daren't dare to dream.

"England is such a nice country and a huge footballing nation," she said ahead of the tournament. "England are much further ahead when it comes to women's football. It's more visible in England, and they have a very strong league. It feels like there's a real appetite for women's football here."

The sense of collective purpose instilled into them by Wiegman and a groundswell of public affection saw them prevail.

Eight-time winners Germany had no answer to what England brought to Wembley. The near 88,000-strong crowd serenaded the players and the coach afterwards with their anthem Sweet Caroline, just as they had done every step of the way, and this one felt all the sweeter.

England scored 22 goals en route to the title – now a tournament record. They finished with a perfect record, winning every game they played. Wiegman, in turn, became the first person to lead two different countries to the European title.

HISTORY MADE. SOCIETY CHANGED.

And now Wiegman is the reigning UEFA Women's Coach of the Year, adding to the two FIFA Coach of the Year titles already accrued.

"This award is really for everyone involved with the England team, The FA, the staff and of course, most of all, the players. Thank you very much," she said upon receipt of her award.

"Things have been set in place and gone very well since I started with the team in September. We've really enjoyed it and we've performed at our highest level. Our fans have been great too, so thank you to all of them for supporting us so much."

Next up is the main trophy that has so far eluded her. The World Cup. England finished their qualifying campaign with 10 wins out of 10, 80 goals scored and precisely zero conceded. The tournament will take place in Australia and New Zealand with England surely to be counted among the favourites alongside the USWNT and Brazil as well as the European countries.

England will be hungry to add to their titles. After all, the European Championship should come to be seen as the start of the Wiegman era and not the end.

Whatever happens, her journey to the pinnacle of the game is complete. The only questions are how much more can she achieve? And if Wiegman can change society all over again...

Team player: Personal awards have been plentiful for Wiegman but she's always keen to emphasise the collective effort that brings success

ENGLAND 2022
ENGLAND 2022

OUR HEROES

The 23 players who helped England bring it home in the most successful UEFA Women's EURO ever

OUR YEAR
1

GOALKEEPER

MARY EARPS

Mary Earps' post-match dancing on a press conference table is arguably one of the most iconic images in English football. But by her own admission, Earps' journey to European Championship winner "hasn't been easy."

Fully deserving of her spot in the official EURO 2022 Team of the Tournament, Earps won major plaudits for her role in England's success after conceding just two goals across the duration of the tournament.

However, the Manchester United shot-stopper only solidified her place as her country's first-choice goalkeeper upon Sarina Wiegman's appointment. Having previously admitted, "I made peace with not being an England player any longer," her international career appeared to be over. Nonetheless, she was handed her first appearance in almost two years in Wiegman's first game as head coach and has made the position her own despite strong competition from Ellie Roebuck and Hannah Hampton.

Born in Nottingham, a future between the sticks was destiny for Earps from just 10 years of age when she made an instant impact for local club West Bridgford Colts, explaining: "In the first game that I played with West Bridgford Colts, we were rotating keepers and I went in goal for a stint – I saved a penalty and I never came out of goal after that."

Earps has developed a wealth of experience throughout her domestic career, initially appearing in the inaugural WSL season for Doncaster Rovers Belles. Part-time jobs, including one in a cinema, were a necessity as she attempted to make the petrol money needed to drive to training. A far cry from the success that would follow.

She made her UEFA Women's Champions League debut as a 20-year-old for Birmingham City in 2013, before returning to the European stage in 2018 when opting to sign for defending Bundesliga champions VfL Wolfsburg after leaving Reading. She helped the German side register their third consecutive domestic double during the 2018-19 season.

A move back home beckoned when Earps signed for the newly-promoted Red Devils under Casey Stoney, debuting for her current club in the 2019 Manchester derby in front of 31,000 supporters. She was rewarded with a new contract in 2021, signing a deal until 2023 at Old Trafford.

Admirably, Earps has also made strides both on and off the field during her

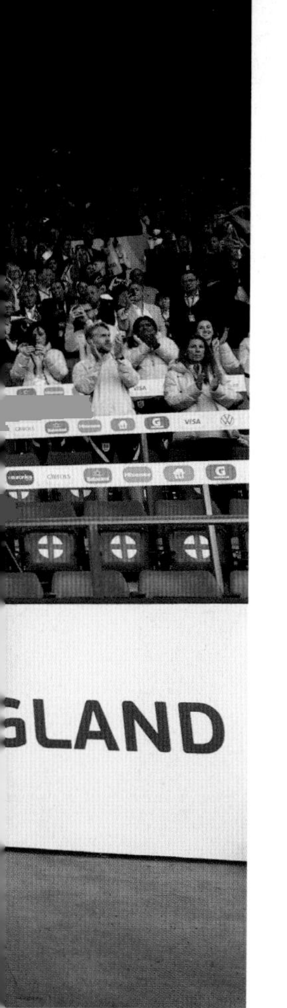

"IN THE FIRST GAME I PLAYED WE WERE ROTATING KEEPERS. I SAVED A PENALTY AND I NEVER CAME OUT OF GOAL AFTER THAT"

professional career. Between 2012 and 2016, she studied Information Management and Business Studies at Loughborough University and graduated with an upper second-class honours degree. Despite revealing that "I eat, sleep, dream and breathe football," her entrepreneurial interests are also clear.

Representing England at under-17, under-19, and under-23 levels, Earps finally won her first cap in a 4-0 friendly win over Switzerland in Biel. She played every minute of the EUROs and kept the joint-most clean sheets alongside Germany's Merle Frohms, who coincidentally vacated the space that Earps would fill at Wolfsburg. Her save to deny Sofia Jakobsson inside the opening 30 seconds of the 4-0 semi-final win against Sweden saw comparisons drawn to fellow United 'keeper David De Gea, who sent messages of congratulations throughout the summer.

STATS

DOB: 7/3/1993	England debut: 10/6/2017 v Switzerland
Club: Manchester United	UEFA EURO 2022 apps: 6
Position: Goalkeeper	UEFA EURO 2022 clean sheets: 4

6

DEFENDER

MILLIE BRIGHT

Towering headers, goal-line blocks, crucial interceptions, imposing physicality, eye-catching passes and dribbles out of defence, England vice-captain Millie Bright excels at everything you could ask for in a central defender.

Bright was the cornerstone of Sarina Wiegman's back-line on the road to European glory, playing a vital role in the Championship's best defence which conceded only two goals across the entire competition.

Bright is equally adept at providing a threat in attack as she is dominating in defence. With only six minutes of play remaining against Spain in the quarter-final, England found themselves trailing and in need of a goal when Wiegman turned to Bright in an attempt to find one. This would have come as a surprise to some, but not to those who caught a glimpse of England's Arnold Clark Cup win against Germany in February where she was deployed as a makeshift striker, with her aerial presence causing mayhem among defenders. On that night, Bright struck the match-winning goal to claim the competition's Golden Boot and she certainly contributed to a dramatic turnaround against La Roja in Brighton by occupying defenders to make space for Alessia Russo and Ella Toone, the latter netting a late leveller.

Such versatility and attributes mean Bright is a valuable asset to both club and country. Nonetheless, having first sat on a horse at the age of two, an equestrian career

had initially seemed destiny for the Chesterfield-born star after she progressed to compete in dressage and showjumping at county level and worked as a groom for a leading dressage rider after leaving school.

To the delight of Emma Hayes and Chelsea, who she stars for nowadays, football was Bright's choice as she overcame a serious childhood battle with asthma to join Sheffield United's academy before moving to Doncaster Rovers Belles in 2009. She sealed a move to the Blues in 2014 having been shortlisted for the Women's Super League 2 Player of the Year award. In her first campaign at the club, Bright helped Chelsea claim the WSL title and was named Chelsea Players' Player of the Year by her team-mates. Despite missing out on retaining their crown the following season, international recognition would shortly follow as Bright made her England debut in 2016.

Having regained their league crown in 2017, Bright has been a leading figure in Chelsea's impressive record of winning five of the last six WSL titles. She penned a new deal at the club in 2018 and has won two FA Cups as well as two League Cups since doing so. Bright featured in the FIFA Best XI in both 2020 and 2021.

'BRIGHT WAS THE CORNERSTONE OF SARINA WIEGMAN'S BACK-LINE ON THE ROAD TO EUROPEAN GLORY, PLAYING A VITAL ROLE IN THE CHAMPIONSHIP'S BEST DEFENCE'

Behind Bright's magnificent EURO 2022 campaign was a burning desire to atone for previous regrets. Having been named by Phil Neville in the squad for the 2019 World Cup in France, Bright appeared in the majority of group matches as well as in the round of 16 and quarter-final. However, she was sent off as England fell to defeat against the USA in the semi-final. She admitted earlier this summer that failure "gives you motivation and that little bit of fire inside you when you need it."

STATS

DOB: 21/08/1993	England debut: 20/09/2016 v Belgium
Club: Chelsea	UEFA EURO 2022 apps: 6
Position: Defender	UEFA EURO 2022 goals: 0

4

MIDFIELDER

KEIRA WALSH

It's safe to say the summer of 2022 was a rather hectic one for Keira Walsh.

The Rochdale-born midfield maestro was vital to England's success in July before securing a world-record fee move to Barcelona just a month later from Manchester City.

Now regarded as one of the best midfielders in the world, Walsh signed a three-year deal with the Spanish giants, who are a force to be feared on the European stage. And by adding Walsh to their ranks, the Catalan club, who were Champions League runners-up last season, will only go from strength to strength.

Walsh broke through into the City first team back in 2014 at just 17 years old when she made her FA Women's Super League debut off the bench in a 1-0 win over Notts County.

Since that campaign, Walsh has gone on to become a regular fixture at the heart of City's midfield.

During her time in Manchester, Walsh enjoyed a trophy-laden spell with City, which saw them claim the 2016 FA Women's Super League title, three FA Cups and four League Cups. She made 211 appearances for the club, scoring eight goals.

At just 25, she had already amassed 50 caps for England and was also part of the Great Britain side that reached the quarter-final of the 2020 Tokyo Olympic Games.

At international level, Walsh was selected for the England Under-15s at just 12 years old back in November 2009.

From there, she progressed through the England age groups, featuring for the Under-17s, Under-19s and Under-23s on the international stage.

Then in November 2017, she received her first senior team call-up, which incidentally, was also England captain Leah Williamson's first call-up.

After making her international debut in a 5-0 thrashing of Kazakhstan, Walsh has become a mainstay for England.

Following her Lionesses debut, the then 21-year-old midfielder was handed the captain's armband for another clash against Kazakhstan, which England went on to win 6-0.

Walsh was also instrumental in helping England to win the 2019 SheBelieves Cup, which saw England pitted against the United States, Japan and Brazil in a group-format tournament.

Then, later that year, Walsh was heavily involved in England's incredible run to the 2019 World Cup semi-final, as they were narrowly defeated 2-1 by the US.

'THE MIDFIELDER PLAYED A STARRING ROLE DURING EURO 2022, OOZING CLASS AT EVERY STAGE. SHE PLAYED ALL BUT FIVE MINUTES OF ENGLAND'S GAMES'

Fast forward three years, and England were ready to put their World Cup heartbreak behind them with Walsh on hand to help Wiegman's side overcome their doubters.

The midfielder played a starring role during EURO 2022, oozing class at every stage. She played all but five minutes of England's games and provided the assist for Ella Toone's opener against Germany in the final.

Her impressive performances were recognised when she was included in UEFA's Team of the Tournament. The world is every bit her oyster.

STATS

DOB: 08/04/1997	England debut: 28/11/2017 v Kazakhstan
Club: Barcelona	UEFA EURO 2022 apps: 6
Position: Midfielder	UEFA EURO 2022 goals: 0

FORWARD

NIKITA PARRIS

While Nikita Parris only made two appearances at EURO 2022 this summer, she is determined to leave a lasting legacy from her England career. A diminutive attacker with the ability to ease past defenders and an eye for goal, Parris has been at the heart of England's success across the last few years since debuting in 2016.

Parris struck her first goal in an international competition five years ago, netting the winner in England's 2–1 group stage win against Portugal at the European Championship. She would finish qualifying for the 2019 FIFA Women's World Cup as the top scorer before going on to make an impact on the competition in France. Having been handed the number seven shirt for the tournament, Parris' place in the squad was revealed by David Beckham. In the opening group game against Scotland, Parris scored her first World Cup goal in a 2-1 win and was named FIFA's Player of the Match.

A valued member of the squad, Parris featured twice at EURO 2022, coming off the bench in the quarter-final win against Spain and the victory over Germany in the final.

Having begun to play football at just six years of age, Parris' passion for the game was clear when she created her very own female football team named Kingsley United, alongside her sister and two cousins.

Aged 14, Parris joined Everton's Centre of Excellence, where one coach revealed her

"pace and physical presence stood out," and she made her senior debut for the club just two years later in 2010. Parris featured in the UEFA Women's Champions League later that year, scoring a brace in the Toffees' 10–0 qualifying win over Borec.

A breakout season followed in 2013 when Parris scored six goals in 11 games, including a brace in the Merseyside derby against her childhood club Liverpool. She went even better the next campaign as Parris netted 11 times in 19 games despite Everton's relegation, subsequently being selected for the WSL Team of the Year.

In a bid to contend for an international jersey, Parris returned to the WSL with Manchester City, where she converted her loan move into a permanent one in 2016. She was a prominent figure as City claimed the WSL title in emphatic style, going the season unbeaten and only conceding four goals. Parris won the 2017 FA Cup with City and registered 11 goals during the 2017-18 WSL season including a hat-trick against Yeovil Town.

The 2018-19 season saw Parris exhibit outstanding goalscoring form. She found the back of the net 19 times, becoming the highest all-time WSL goalscorer and registering

'A DIMINUTIVE ATTACKER WITH THE ABILITY TO EASE PAST DEFENDERS AND AN EYE FOR GOAL, PARRIS HAS BEEN AT THE HEART OF ENGLAND'S SUCCESS FOR THE PAST SIX YEARS'

the second-most assists. It was little surprise that she was voted as the Football Writers' Association Women's Player of the Year.

Parris signed for Olympique Lyonnais in June 2019 and scored eight times before COVID-19 cut the domestic campaign short. She would, however, win her first-ever Champions League title that season, with a victory against VfL Wolfsburg that season which she missed through suspension. Another 11 goals followed a season later before Arsenal paid a club-record fee for her services.

Parris signed for Manchester United in the August following European glory in 2022.

STATS

DOB: 10/03/1994	England debut: 04/06/2016 v Serbia
Club: Manchester United	UEFA EURO 2022 apps: 2
Position: Forward	UEFA EURO 2022 goals: 0

12

DEFENDER

JESS CARTER

Having admitted that she never dreamed of becoming a professional football player as she only knew "one or two female footballers," being part of the team that won England's first ever European Championship trophy was hailed as an "indescribable feeling" by Jess Carter.

The Warwick-born defender came on as a 74th-minute substitute for Lucy Bronze in the 5-0 group stage win against Northern Ireland and has been described as one of the "best one-v-one defenders in the country" by her Chelsea boss Emma Hayes.

Born to an American father and English mother, Carter grew up located just five minutes away from her first team, Birmingham City, and captained Warwick Juniors to County Cup success prior to joining the club's academy in 2013. She also played rugby union for Worcester Warriors as a child.

Her debut arrived on the European stage in a 2013-14 UEFA Women's Champions League quarter-final against Arsenal, where she would impressively be named player of the match. She was part of a Birmingham side that reached a League Cup final and Women's FA Cup final in 2016 and 2017 respectively. Subsequently, her performances would see Carter win the 2017 PFA Women's Young Player of the Year and earn international recognition.

Considered a versatile player with the ability to perform in a number of different roles

across the back line, Carter signed for Chelsea a year later but struggled to break into an established defence that had helped the Blues secure a domestic double the previous term.

After scoring her first goal for the club on her only WSL start of the 2019-20 campaign, Carter began to be integrated as a regular starter upon a knee injury to Maren Mjelde. Her performances as a full-back helped Chelsea secure a spot in their first-ever Champions League final, with Carter notably providing a pin-point delivery for Pernille Harder to secure victory in the semi-final.

Carter was rewarded with an extended contract in 2021 and emerged as a vital part of Chelsea's defensive unit on the right-hand side of a back three. Her outstanding performance in the FA Cup final victory against Arsenal ensured her side sealed an unprecedented domestic quadruple. The club's most recent WSL crown would signify the biggest role Carter has played in a title-winning campaign.

Despite featuring on only one occasion during EURO 2022, Carter embraced her role as a squad member after her experience of remaining patient to win a starting berth in Hayes' Chelsea team.

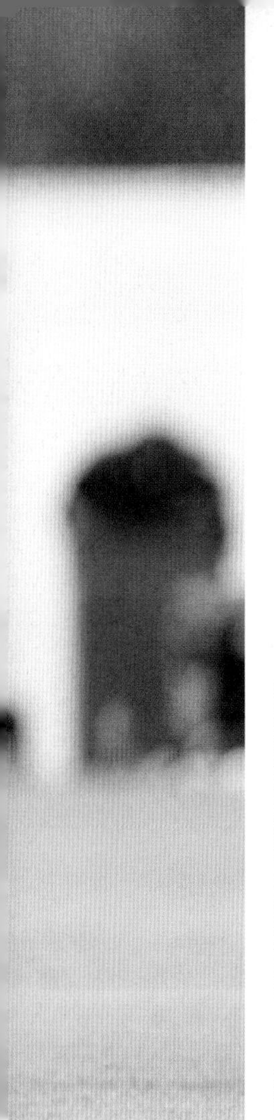

"PART OF OUR SUCCESS, PART OF OUR MOTIVATION, WAS OBVIOUSLY TO INSPIRE PEOPLE AND THAT IS CLEARLY WHAT WE HAVE DONE"

She was a beneficiary of Sarina Wiegman's appointment as England head coach, winning a first cap in four years following on from her international debut in 2017.

Off the field, Carter is known to be an advocate for providing aspiring young players with equal opportunities. She is an ambassador of a London all-girls football academy and revealed a cornerstone of the Lionesses' EURO 2022 win was the squad's desire to provide the role models that Carter could not look up to 20 years ago. "Part of our success, part of our motivation, was obviously to inspire people and that is clearly what we have done," she said.

STATS

DOB: 27/10/1997	England debut: 28/11/2017 v Kazakhstan
Club: Chelsea	UEFA EURO 2022 apps: 1
Position: Defender	UEFA EURO 2022 goals: 0

16

MIDFIELDER

JILL SCOTT

Jill Scott's international contribution stretches far, far beyond the summer of 2022. She is undoubtedly an England legend.

EURO 2022 was Scott's 10th major international competition since debuting in 2006, and while she only played a peripheral role, it seems that her career was destined to end at such a high point. She described European triumph as a "forever moment."

Scott announced her retirement in the aftermath of the tournament's conclusion, with tributes from the Duke and Duchess of Cambridge demonstrating how highly regarded she is after years of dedication to her country, as does the MBE she was awarded in the 2020 New Year Honours for services to women's football.

Having graduated through Sunderland's academy, Scott made her debut for the club in 2004 and would win the Women's Player of the Month Award for September, aged only 18. Such is her talent, Scott would receive her first senior England call-up aged just 19, and debuted three months later in a 4-0 win over the Netherlands.

She would soon swap Sunderland for Everton, where Scott enjoyed a lengthy spell, and received her first taste of an international competition at the 2007 World Cup in China. Scott scored in a 6-1 group stage triumph over Argentina.

In 2009, Scott was among the first-ever group of players to be handed central

contracts, a move that was labelled as a "step in the right direction and a key strategy for England Women," at the time. Later that year, Scott was part of the England team that suffered heartbreak in the 2009 European Championship, after she had scored in a semi-final victory against the Netherlands. She would be the only member of that squad to finish her career with a EURO winner's medal.

Olympic recognition would arrive for Scott in 2012 when she was named in the Great Britain squad to participate in their first Olympic women's football tournament. Scott scored in a 3-0 group stage win over Cameroon.

Having won both the FA Women's Premier League Cup and the FA Women's Cup at Everton, in addition to being voted 2008 FA Players' Player of the Year and 2011 FA International Player of the Year, Scott signed for Manchester City in 2013. She was an integral figure in a City team that went unbeaten during the 2016 WSL and conceded just four goals.

Scott featured at the 2013 and 2017 European Championships and was part of teams that reached the World Cup semi-finals in 2015 and 2019. She made her 150th England

'DESCRIBED AS A "VERY SPECIAL PERSON" BY SARINA WIEGMAN, FORMER TEAM-MATE ALEX GREENWOOD ALSO LABELLED THE 35-YEAR-OLD AS A "TRUE LEGEND"'

appearance against Northern Ireland, in a match where she would play the whole 90 minutes and captain the team.

Off the field, Scott, who was nicknamed 'Crouchy' during her playing days, owns a coffee shop alongside her partner in Manchester. She is already a UEFA 'B' licence holder and is known to harbour aspirations of coaching in the future. Described as a "very special person" by Sarina Wiegman, former team-mate Alex Greenwood also labelled the 35-year-old as a "true legend." Scott also proved hugely popular with supporters who celebrated England's triumph at Trafalgar Square in London, the day after the unforgettable victory at Wembley.

STATS

DOB: 02/02/1987	England debut: 30/08/2006 v Netherlands
Club: Retired (previously Man City)	UEFA EURO 2022 apps: 4
Position: Midfielder	UEFA EURO 2022 goals: 0

21

GOALKEEPER

ELLIE ROEBUCK

Ellie Roebuck found herself behind Mary Earps as Sarina Wiegman's first-choice keeper for the 2022 European Championship, with the latter starting every game of England's stellar campaign.

And while Roebuck did not feature on the pitch for her country during the summer tournament, she was on hand to help the rest of Wiegman's squad prepare for whatever challenges they faced.

A massive Sheffield United fan, Roebuck held a season ticket at Bramall Lane when she was younger, and she names two of her biggest goalkeeping inspirations as former Manchester United star Peter Schmeichel and Italian icon Gianluigi Buffon.

The Sheffield-born shot-stopper came through the ranks at the Blades before making the switch to join Manchester City back in 2016.

Since her arrival at City, Roebuck's career has gone from strength to strength.

While she made her professional debut during the 2016-17 campaign, her real breakthrough opportunity came when she impressed in place of the injured Karen Bardsley during the latter half of the 2017-18 season.

Roebuck starred in goal for City, helping them to secure a top-two finish in the Barclays Women's Super League as well as a spot in the Champions League for a third successive year.

So impressive were her performances in Bardsley's absence, Roebuck became their first-choice 'keeper for the 2018-19 campaign, which saw her make 17 appearances in all competitions for City.

The following season saw her claim the WSL's inaugural Golden Glove award, with Roebuck keeping 10 clean sheets in 16 league appearances.

And the individual recognition for her achievements did not end there. In 2020, Roebuck was one of six nominees for FIFA's The Best Women's Goalkeeper of the Year award.

Her performances for City also earned her an England call-up in October 2018, where she won her first senior international cap after replacing Mary Earps in the 79th minute against Austria. She then made her first competitive England start against Spain in April 2019, which the Lionesses won 2-1.

Of course, Roebuck was no stranger to the England set-up before her senior team debut. The Manchester City keeper made plenty of international appearances at age-grade level, helping England to a third-place finish at the Under-17 European Championship in 2014.

She was also part of the England Under-20s squad that won bronze at the 2018 World Cup in France.

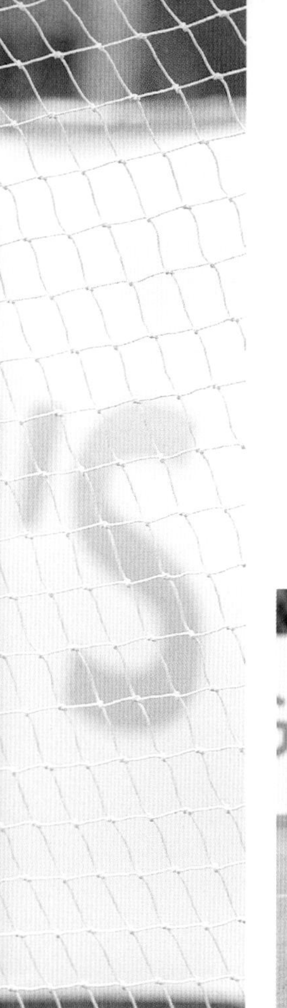

'IN 2020 ROEBUCK WAS ONE OF SIX NOMINEES FOR FIFA'S THE BEST WOMEN'S GOALKEEPER OF THE YEAR AWARD'

Since her international debut back in 2018, Roebuck has gone on to make further appearances for England, and looks set to be involved in the international set-up for years to come.

And Roebuck has also starred on the international stage for Great Britain during the 2020 Olympics in Tokyo. She played all four of Team GB's Olympic matches, which saw Roebuck and co lose out in the quarter-final to Australia.

Following last summer's Olympics, a calf injury restricted her to just 10 WSL appearances for City during the 2021-22 campaign, which hindered her preparations for EURO 2022.

STATS

DOB: 23/09/1999
Club: Manchester City
Position: Goalkeeper

England debut: 08/11/2018 v Austria
UEFA EURO 2022 apps: 0
UEFA EURO 2022 clean sheets: 0

9

STRIKER

ELLEN WHITE

Ellen White excels at doing one thing above all others. Scoring goals. She retired in August as England's top female goalscorer and second-highest goalscorer of all time with 52 international goals. Nevertheless, being labelled as a "true leader of women" by The FA's women's football director, Sue Campbell, paints an even truer picture of White.

Her contribution to European Championship glory was vital, starting every match of the campaign and being singled out by Sarina Wiegman for being "the perfect team player" and helping "younger players to find their way in international football." It has since been revealed that White had even battled back from a punctured lung to lead her country to success.

Wiegman has also described White's finishing ability as "world-class," evident in England's record 8-0 win against Norway where she netted a brace. Having scored a magnificent goal at the 2011 World Cup against Japan, England fans have grown accustomed to White's incredible attacking instinct since her international debut in 2010. She would later be voted as England Women's Player of the Year. While White struggled for goals at the 2013 European Championship and 2015 World Cup, she scored in a 6-0 win over Scotland at EURO 2017 and undoubtedly stamped her authority on the 2019 World Cup in France.

White began the tournament with a goal, against Scotland once more, before netting a brace against holders Japan in a 2-0 victory. She carried her form into the knock-out stages, scoring against Cameroon in a feisty clash and against Norway in the quarter-final. The latter strike saw White become England's top goalscorer in Women's World Cups.

Her display in the semi-final against considerable favourites USA was also to be admired. Despite falling 2-0 down, the Aylesbury-born attacker pulled one back early and was harshly denied a vital equaliser by VAR. She also won a penalty that captain Steph Houghton failed to convert and ended the competition as joint-top goalscorer. White gained her 100th cap for England against Austria in November 2021 and scored the only goal in a 1–0 win.

From a domestic perspective, White was scouted by Arsenal when playing for local club Aylesbury Town. Yet, she would move to Chelsea as a 16-year-old and would become the Blues' top scorer for three seasons. Following time at Leeds United, which included a League Cup win, White returned to Arsenal, helping the Gunners win three league titles and two FA Cups within three years.

'SHE WAS SINGLED OUT BY SARINA WIEGMAN FOR BEING "THE PERFECT TEAM PLAYER" AND HELPING "YOUNGER PLAYERS TO FIND THEIR WAY IN INTERNATIONAL FOOTBALL"'

She would then enjoy spells with Notts County and Birmingham City before signing for Manchester City in 2019. With the club she became the second player in WSL history to reach 50 goals and eventually became the record goalscorer in the WSL, having scored 55 times. Vivianne Miedema would go on to claim the record.

Though White did not foresee herself hanging up her boots at 33, she claimed upon retirement: "My dreams came true on July 31, winning the EUROs and becoming a European champion."

STATS

DOB: 09/05/1989	England debut: 25/03/2010 v Austria
Club: Retired (previously Man City)	UEFA EURO 2022 apps: 6
Position: Striker	UEFA EURO 2022 goals: 2

OUR YEAR
22

DEFENDER

LOTTE WUBBEN-MOY

Lotte Wubben-Moy admirably battled back from COVID-19 to play a part in Sarina Wiegman's victorious squad. Providing valuable depth and competition to England's defensive unit, Wubben-Moy's path to becoming an international footballer can be likened to that of fellow defender and team-mate Demi Stokes.

Born to English and Dutch parents, Wubben-Moy comes from a family with a strong sporting background. Her father, an accomplished mountain biker and velodrome cyclist, would take part in a competitive stage of the Tour de France each year, while her sister was a high-achieving ballerina up until the age of 17. Wubben-Moy herself played goal defence in netball, enjoyed the long jump and was an 800m runner during her younger days.

Yet, her passion for football was clear when growing up in Bow where she became known as 'the girl that played football,' a phrase that Wubben-Moy takes great pride in being heard less and less nowadays. Alongside friends and a teacher, she created a local 5-a-side girls' football team, which she credits for later being scouted by the likes of West Ham, aged nine, and Millwall two years later.

Fascinatingly, Wubben-Moy initially begun her footballing journey as a striker, even becoming top scorer during her time with the Hammers. She began moving backwards in positions and settled as a centre-back when she signed for childhood club Arsenal as

a teenager, but has since gone on record to explain: "I just wanted to play football, where on the pitch that was didn't matter!"

Wubben-Moy was just 16 when the Gunners handed her a first senior appearance in 2015, coming on in a 2–1 WSL win over Notts County. She formed a small part of the team that won a domestic cup double, claiming League Cup and Women's FA Cup titles. After helping the club go unbeaten during the 2017 FA WSL Spring Series, Arsenal offered Wubben-Moy the opportunity to sign professional terms later that year.

In her own words, going from playing on a concrete cage pitch in East London to being wanted by one of the biggest women's teams in the country was "a dream come true," but similarly to Stokes, she made the bold call to pursue further education and accept a scholarship at the University of North Carolina in the USA where she would play for North Carolina Tar Heels, describing the decision as "one of the hardest decisions I have ever had to make in my life."

Coincidentally, joining Wubben-Moy at UNC would be future Lionesses team-mate Alessia Russo. While missing out on WSL action, the physical nature of football in America would complement Wubben-Moy's technical foundations that had been laid with the Gunners.

With COVID-19 drastically affecting schedules, Wubben-Moy made an emotional return to Arsenal by signing a professional contract. With an impressive passing range and ability to read the game, she quickly became an integral part of teams under both Joe Montemurro and Jonas Eidevall.

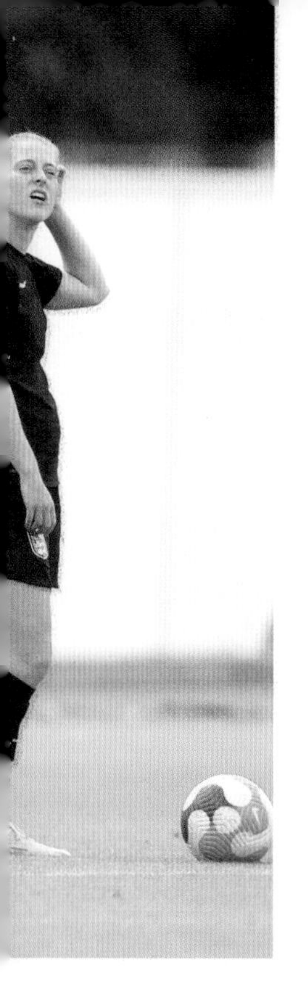

"I JUST WANTED TO PLAY FOOTBALL. WHERE ON THE PITCH THAT WAS DIDN'T MATTER"

STATS

DOB: 11/1/1999	England debut: 23/2/2021 v Northern Ireland
Club: Arsenal	UEFA EURO 2022 apps: 0
Position: Defender	UEFA EURO 2022 goals: 0

10

MIDFIELDER

GEORGIA STANWAY

If there was one person who knew Georgia Stanway would nail her superb match-winning strike in England's 2-1 quarter-final win over Spain, it was Joanne Stanway, who stood in goal when her daughter practised shooting as a 15-year-old. That practice would certainly prove perfect, as Stanway emulated childhood hero Alan Shearer with an explosive finish to send her country into the final four.

Having trailed for much of the encounter, Stanway's extra-time goal in Brighton felt like a pivotal moment in England's triumphant campaign. As a key figure of Sarina Wiegman's squad, the Newcastle-supporting star's quality shone through when her team needed it most.

Despite being just 23 at EURO 2022, supporters are now accustomed to Stanway's presence in England line-ups after she debuted in 2018 as a 19-year-old. Her early career was spent as a striker before moving to an attacking midfield position and now into the box-to-box role she currently occupies. Such versatility is indicative of Stanway's team-first mentality which has even seen her go on record to joke "I'd play in goal if I had to."

By her own admission, Stanway claims she is "most at ease when I'm playing with a smile," leading to former boss Phil Neville encouraging her to play as she would on a Cumbrian park. Manchester City manager Gareth Taylor has likened Stanway to a "wind-up toy" such is her enthusiasm on the pitch. Stanway has revealed that level of

commitment to the cause means "I can be a bit nasty," after she grew up enjoying the "rough and tumble" that came with playing alongside boys as a child.

As a youngster, Stanway displayed talent as a cricketer but opted to give up the sport to focus on training with Blackburn Rovers. Before making a senior appearance for the Lancashire club, Stanway signed for Manchester City in 2016, where she would debut in the WSL as a 16-year-old. A season later, Stanway's long-range effort against Sunderland beat the likes of Sergio Aguero, Kevin De Bruyne, Yaya Toure and Toni Duggan to win the club's Goal of the Year award, a hint of what would follow later in her career.

Stanway was part of a City side that went unbeaten throughout the WSL season, winning the title with a defensive unit that conceded just four goals. Her performances across the 2017–18 season saw Stanway named in the UEFA Women's Champions League Team of the Season, while she was voted as the PFA Women's Young Player of the Year the following campaign.

After netting a hat trick in an 8–0 win against Nottingham Forest earlier this year, Stanway became the club's highest women's scorer after leapfrogging England team-

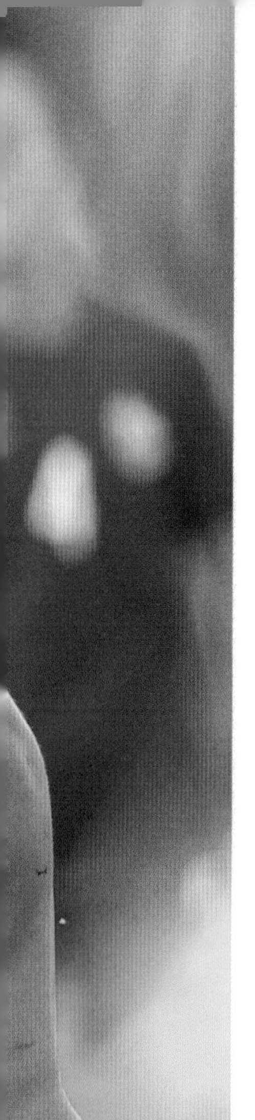

'MANCHESTER CITY MANAGER GARETH TAYLOR HAS LIKENED HER TO A "WIND-UP TOY" SUCH IS HER ENTHUSIASM ON THE PITCH'

mate Nikita Parris on the goalscoring charts. A seven-year spell with the Sky Blues came to an end in May 2022 when Stanway agreed a three-year deal with Bayern Munich, where she will link up with several members of the German team that were defeated in the final.

With a goal-laden tournament and the immense celebrations that followed, fans could be forgiven for forgetting that Stanway netted England's opener in the 8-0 hammering of Norway to set the Lionesses on their path to EURO glory.

STATS

DOB: 03/01/1999	England debut: 08/11/2018 v Austria
Club: Bayern Munich	UEFA EURO 2022 apps: 6
Position: Midfielder	UEFA EURO 2022 goals: 2

19

FORWARD

BETHANY ENGLAND

The appropriately-named Bethany England could not have wished for a better first major tournament at senior level. England's rise from working in her local chippy to becoming a European champion acts as a major source of inspiration to any young footballer.

Having received her first senior international call-up in 2019, England has become a regular feature of squads in the time since and reached double figures for goals with a brace in the 10-0 triumph over Luxembourg in September. She averages a goal every two games for her country.

Like many of her team-mates, England has overcome several challenges in order to don the Three Lions. After playing in a boys' team during her junior years, she was scouted by Sheffield United to join their girls' centre of excellence alongside her sister Laura. She would soon join Doncaster Rovers Belles alongside future England and Chelsea team-mate Millie Bright.

Not only was England required to work part-time jobs to fulfil her dream of playing the game on a full-time basis – as many female footballers once were – she also balanced the time with studying for her A-Levels. She has previously explained: "I've done all sorts. I've worked in a bakery, a factory, I've worked at M&S and I've worked in an Indian restaurant."

England was part of the Doncaster team that featured in the inaugural 2011 WSL campaign when the league had semi-professional status. While the club were relegated as part of a league restructure at the end of the 2013 season, England was a beneficiary of second-tier football and registered 14 goals in 2015 to win promotion. Despite being offered a professional contract, a move to reigning WSL champions Chelsea would follow.

Her first season with Chelsea saw England deployed at left wing-back, a far cry from leading the line as she does nowadays. A loan spell at Liverpool in 2017 helped her find form in the top division, scoring 10 goals for the Merseyside club. The temporary move alerted Chelsea manager Emma Hayes to England's goalscoring instincts and she would go on to finish as the Blues' top scorer across the next season.

The following campaign would see England go one better as she scored 14 goals in 15 games, becoming the country's top scorer in all competitions across the top two divisions, and the Super League's second-highest goalscorer. Hayes would later claim that England was the "best English number nine," with her goals sealing League Cup and WSL titles.

'ENGLAND'S RISE FROM WORKING IN A LOCAL CHIPPY TO BECOMING A EUROPEAN CHAMPION ACTS AS A MAJOR SOURCE OF INSPIRATION FOR ANY YOUNG FOOTBALLER'

On an individual basis, she was named the league's Player of the Season and won Player of the Month awards in January and February.

Twelve goals in all competitions, including a first in the UEFA Women's Champions League, throughout the 2020-21 season helped Chelsea become the first female team to secure a domestic quadruple. England still maintains her humble roots nevertheless, admitting that she felt "very lucky and privileged that the hard work put in has paid off."

England didn't feature on the pitch at UEFA Women's EURO 2022 but remains a valued member of Wiegman's squad.

STATS

DOB: 03/06/1994	England debut: 29/08/2019 v Belgium
Club: Chelsea	UEFA EURO 2022 apps: 0
Position: Forward	UEFA EURO 2022 goals: 0

3

DEFENDER

RACHEL DALY

Harrogate-born Rachel Daly played an instrumental role in England's success in the summer, playing in every EURO 2022 match at left-back.

Perhaps one of the most impressive parts of her game is Daly's ability to perform in a number of different positions at a high level, as she is often either deployed at full-back or upfront.

Daly's path to England stardom took her across the pond to St. John's University in New York, where she played collegiate 'soccer' for the St. John's Red Storm after choosing to leave Lincoln Ladies.

A decorated college career saw Daly enter the 2016 National Women's Soccer League draft, where she was selected sixth overall by the Houston Dash.

While domestic success seemingly evaded the Dash, they did manage to win the 2020 NWSL Challenge Cup, which was introduced to mark the league's return following the COVID-19 pandemic.

Daly starred for the Dash during the Challenge Cup, with her being named as the competition's Most Valuable Player in what was Houston's first ever trophy win.

In September 2020, Daly joined West Ham United on loan until the turn of the year. The switch proved to be successful, with Daly bagging five goals in 12 appearances for the Hammers before returning stateside.

After spending the majority of her professional career out in America, Daly is now back in England, having signed for Aston Villa in the summer of 2022.

On the international stage, Daly, like many, has represented her country across a number of age levels.

Having played for England at Under-15, Under-17, Under-19 and Under-23 level, it seemed as though it would only be a matter of time before she was involved with the senior side.

But while she was first called up to the England squad back in December 2013, it was not until the summer of June 2016 when she made her debut in a 7-0 win over Serbia. It was certainly an evening to remember, with Daly – playing upfront – getting on the scoresheet.

Despite her involvement with the England squad, she was not selected as part of Mark Sampson's EURO 2017 squad, which left her yearning to improve her game.

Phil Neville's arrival as England boss in 2018, however, saw Daly return to the international fold for the SheBelieves Cup.

Under Neville, Daly became an England regular, making 26 appearances for the

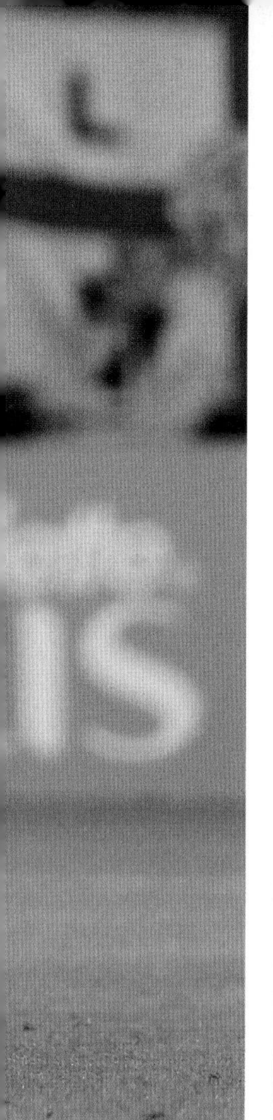

'PERHAPS ONE OF THE MOST IMPRESSIVE PARTS OF HER GAME IS DALY'S ABILITY TO PERFORM IN A NUMBER OF DIFFERENT POSITIONS AT A HIGH LEVEL'

Lionesses between 2018 and 2019, which also saw her feature at the 2019 World Cup in France.

She also played a major part in Hege Riise's Great Britain side at the Tokyo 2020 Olympics, with Daly featuring in all of Team GB's matches on their impressive run to the quarter-final.

Daly underlined her importance to England this summer and having battled her way back into the England fold, you would be hard pushed to bet against the versatile star sticking around for some time to come.

STATS

DOB: 06/12/1991	England debut: 04/06/2016 v Serbia
Club: Aston Villa	UEFA EURO 2022 apps: 6
Position: Defender	UEFA EURO 2022 goals: 0

GERMANY
23 FEBRUARY 2022

PERFECTLY PREPARED

It's hard to imagine a better build-up to a major tournament than the few months England experienced before UEFA Women's EURO 2022.

Having qualified automatically for the finals as hosts, and with a head coach still fairly new to the role, it was important that Sarina Wiegman's side had plenty of training and match time to make sure they would be in the best possible condition by the time they faced Austria in their opening group match in July.

England had eight matches in 2022 before their EURO opener at Old Trafford. A mix of competitive Arnold Clark Cup games, FIFA World Cup qualifying matches and some friendlies gave Wiegman plenty of opportunity to put her plans in place.

The Arnold Clark Cup would see England face three other teams from the top 10 in the world with a competitive edge guaranteed.

First up in the group-format tournament was Canada and Millie Bright's goal earned a 1-1 draw before a stalemate with Spain.

The final match resulted in a satisfying 3-1 win over Germany. Ellen White put England ahead, Lina Magull equalised, and then two late goals from Bright and Fran Kirby at Molineux earned top spot and the trophy on goal difference from Spain.

With silverware in the cabinet, England bounced into two away World Cup qualifiers.

The first, in North Macedonia, allowed the forwards to build their confidence as Beth Mead hit four and Ella Toone got a hat-trick in a 10-0 win.

Four days later, England faced Northern Ireland for the first time in 2022, in Windsor Park. Lauren Hemp broke the deadlock in the first half and added a second after the break with a Georgia Stanway double and another from Toone earning a 5-0 victory.

Winning the Arnold Clark Cup was a key part of a challenging build-up to the main event of 2022 – and helped foster team spirit along the way

A 5-1 victory over European champions the Netherlands showed what England were capable of, while Jill Scott (right) scored the final goal against Switzerland which wrapped up a good few months of preparation

The month before EURO 2022 got underway, England faced three teams who had also qualified for the finals, including the reigning champions.

First up were Belgium, who put up a stern challenge, before Chloe Kelly's deflected shot opened the scoring, closely followed by a Rachel Daly effort. A late own goal secured a 3-0 win.

The result at Elland Road the following week really got the home fans excited. EURO 2017 winners, the Netherlands, took the lead midway through the first half before Lucy Bronze made sure it was level at the break.

The second half was all about England as a Mead double, and one each for Toone and Hemp sealed an emphatic 5-1 win.

England's final engagement before EURO 2022 was another impressive win, this time in Switzerland.

Again, it took time for England to break down their opponents before second-half strikes from Alessia Russo, a Stanway penalty, Bethany England and Jill Scott made it 4-0.

"We always have things to improve," said Wiegman after the game. "I think we are in a very good place. These are all friendlies and it's very nice to play and to learn from them. But it really starts next Wednesday.

"We are in a very good place."

England scored 31 goals in eight games in 2022 before the beginning of UEFA Women's EURO 2022 to ensure confidence was high before facing the best teams in Europe

THE QUALIFIERS

The other 15 places at UEFA Women's EURO 2022 were decided by qualifying matches with nine countries going through as group winners and three qualifying as best-performing runners-up. Six countries would fight it out for the final three places through play-off matches. Despite winning their decider, the conflict in Ukraine meant Russia were replaced by Portugal.

The other 15 qualifying teams:

Netherlands	GW
Denmark	GW
Norway	GW
Spain	GW
Finland	GW
Sweden	GW
France	GW
Belgium	GW
Germany	GW
Italy	GR
Iceland	GR
Austria	GR
N Ireland	PO
Switzerland	PO
Portugal	PO

GW = group winners
GR = group runners-up
PO = qualified through play-offs

READY TO ROAR

With all the warm-up matches complete, a busy few days before the tournament kick-off included plenty of training, travel and media engagements. As the final preparations were put into place, it was important the build-up was focused but fun...

CRJ1000
BOMBARDIER

POWER
COURAGE

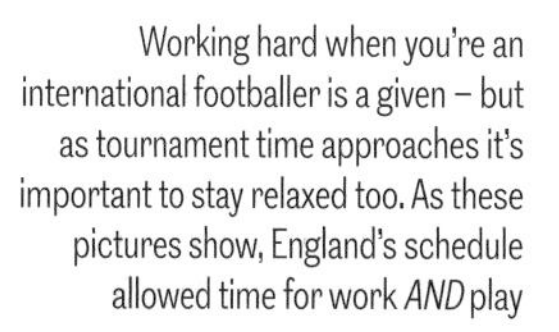

Working hard when you're an international footballer is a given – but as tournament time approaches it's important to stay relaxed too. As these pictures show, England's schedule allowed time for work *AND* play

eat well
M&S

ENGLAND

The spotlight of the country was focused on 23 players and their head coach – but if the pressure was becoming too much, you wouldn't have been able to tell!

WHITE
9

ENGLAND v AUSTRIA
GROUP A - MATCHDAY 1
Old Trafford
6 July 2022

PRE-MATCH BUILD-UP:

"We have waited for the start for such a long time and we can feel that everyone is really ready. Austria is a very strong team, their togetherness is really good and they are a physical and organised team. But if we play our best game we will be on the ball more than they will and we will be able to dominate the game more than they can."

– Sarina Wiegman

"Everyone is really excited. Going into the first game, there is a real buzz around the group and we are all really excited going into it."
– Chloe Kelly

MEAD MAGIC MAKES IT A PERFECT START

The first game of a major tournament – particularly when you are the host nation – is all about getting the three points on the board. That is exactly what England did.

The 1-0 win against Austria was a fantastic occasion on and off the pitch and Sarina Wiegman's players got the job done, even if they weren't at their free-flowing best.

A crowd of 68,871 – a record for a UEFA Women's EURO match – filled Old Trafford with noise and fervour, and they saw Austria put up a strong challenge and start well.

It was England who took the lead in the 16th minute though as Fran Kirby picked out Beth Mead, who lifted the ball delightfully over her Arsenal team-mate Manuela Zingsberger, a VAR check confirming the ball had crossed the line.

An already-excited crowd went wild and the goal settled the home side, who could have been two up just before the break as the Austrian 'keeper denied Lauren Hemp.

England continued to press for a greater advantage in the second half, bringing on Ella Toone, Chloe Kelly and Alessia Russo, but Mary Earps had to be alert at the other end to tip wide a stinging drive from Barbara Dunst.

Irene Fuhrmann's Austria side kept England on their toes and any home nerves could have been settled had Russo or Kelly made more of their chances.

Mead, Kirby and player of the match, Georgia Stanway, gave England plenty of creativity in midfield as the majority of the crowd ultimately went home happy and full of hope for a tournament that promised so much.

A tough encounter provided lots of huff and puff but Beth Mead's early strike was ultimately enough to blow the Austrian house down, to the delight of a packed Old Trafford crowd

10

England 1 Austria 0

Mead 16

England: Earps, Bronze, Bright, Williamson (c), Daly, Stanway, Walsh, Kirby (Toone 63), Mead (Kelly 64), Hemp, White (Russo 64).

Austria: Zinsberger, Wienroither, Wenninger, Schnaderbeck (c) (Georgieva 77), Hanshaw, Puntigam, Naschenweng (Hickelsberger-Füller 59), Feiersinger (Höbinger 87), Zadrazil, Dunst, Billa.

UEFA Player of the Match: Georgia Stanway

ENGLAND 2022

POST-MATCH:

"I think we were a little rushed in the final third. We did create lots of chances but the final touch or choice, we can do that better. But the most important thing is we scored one and kept a clean sheet to get the three points."

– Sarina Wiegman

"I thought we dealt well with the pressure. It took us eight to ten minutes to settle into the game, but we did well and I think we dealt well with the external pressure that was put on us. From a captain's perspective, I think the girls are in a good place."

– Leah Williamson

"It was hard to hear from the sidelines, it was hard to hear Keira [Walsh] behind me, it shows where we're at, that's the standard the fans have set. Bring the noise, it can rattle the opposition."

– Georgia Stanway

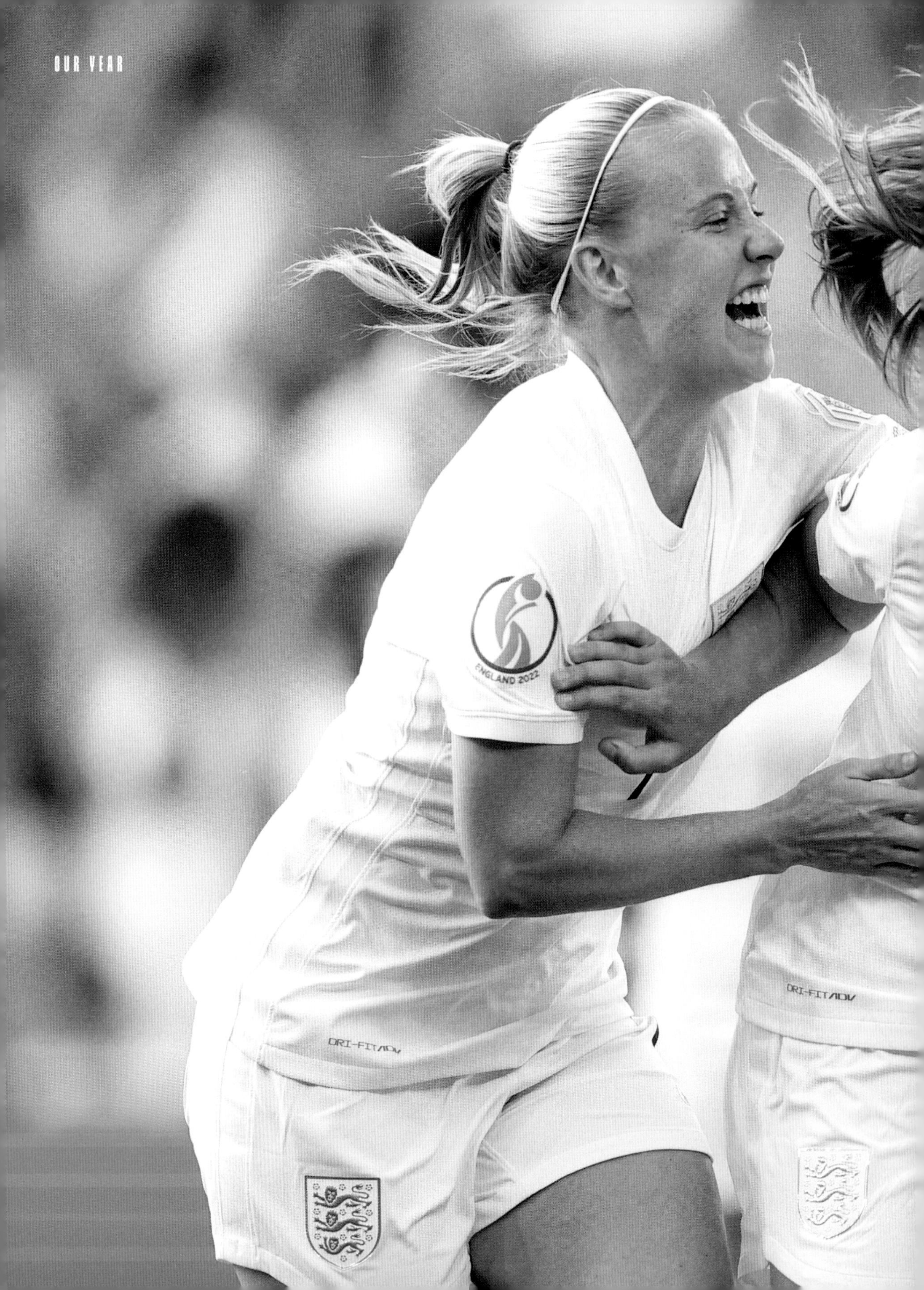
ENGLAND 2022
DRI-FIT ADV
DRI-FIT ADV

ENGLAND v NORWAY
GROUP A - MATCHDAY 2
Brighton & Hove Community Stadium
11 July 2022
NORWAY
11 JULY 2022

PRE-MATCH BUILD-UP:

"We always prepare the same way for our opponents. Some players know who is on the [other side of the] pitch as they work every day with each other.

"[Norway coach Sjogren] wants to attack and we want to too. It's true that when you have the ball the opponent can't score a goal. And when we have the ball, you can score a goal. So if we both want to play an attacking game, then I think it's going to be a real open game, which the fans in the stands will like, I think.

"If we win it we will probably go on to top the group, yes. That would be nice."

– Sarina Wiegman

"Norway are a really good team and are so well respected. They've got some great individual players and collectively they've done well in the past. But we've got such a talented pool of players we should just focus on our journey."

– Rachel Daly

RECORD BREAKERS SHOW FORM OF CHAMPIONS

If England's opening match had been functional, their second group game was simply fantastic.

This was the match that saw Sarina Wiegman's players not only win to secure qualification for the knock-out phase, the margin and manner of victory made the rest of Europe sit up and recognise them as potential champions.

England broke record after record, going 6-0 up by half-time, then adding two more after the break to secure the biggest ever win in a UEFA Women's EURO match with five different players getting on the scoresheet.

The goalscoring began in the 12th minute, Georgia Stanway converting a penalty after Ellen White had been felled in the box. Three minutes later, Lauren Hemp tapped in at the far post after good work from Beth Mead. Then White won the ball back in Norway's half before slotting past Guro Pettersen.

In the 34th minute Hemp returned the earlier compliment by crossing for Mead to head home but the fifth goal was all Mead's work as she dribbled through a shellshocked Norwegian defence to make it 5-0.

When Fran Kirby set up White to add her second in the 41st minute it was already Norway's worst-ever defeat but England were not done yet.

Substitute Alessia Russo headed in Lucy Bronze's second-half cross and in the 81st minute Mead completed her hat-trick when she scored from the rebound following Keira Walsh's strike from outside the area.

To win any match in such a comfortable way at a major tournament is remarkable, but to do it against two-time champions Norway, a team with quality throughout the squad, was more than any England fan would have wished for.

Eng

HEMP
11

7

14

MEAD
7

Georgia Stanway, Lauren Hemp, Ellen White, Beth Mead and Alessia Russo all weighed in with goals as Norway were left shellshocked by a rampant England display

England 8 Norway 0

Stanway 12 (pen)
Hemp 15
White 28, 41
Mead 34, 38, 81
Russo 66

England: Earps, Bronze, Bright, Williamson (c), Daly (Greenwood 57), Stanway (Scott 80), Walsh, Kirby (Toone 57), Mead, Hemp (Kelly 70), White (Russo 57).

Norway: Pettersen, Blakstad, Thorisdottir, Mjelde (c), T Hansen, Syrstad Engen, Bøe Rise (Maanum 59), Reiten (Terland 84), Sævik (Bergsvand 46), Graham Hansen (Eikeland 75), Hegerberg (Ildhusøy 75).

UEFA Player of the Match: Beth Mead

NORWAY
11 JULY 2022
7

UEFA WOMEN'S EURO ENGLAND 2022
MEAD
7
com
Hisens

9

POST-MATCH:

"Whether you win 1-0 or 8-0, you only get three points. We're through the group, so that's really nice; we have the time to prepare for Northern Ireland. I expect that will be a good game too and we're going to have a very good opponent in the quarter-finals, and that's not going to be easy."

– Sarina Wiegman

"We knew today was going to be a tough test and we really rose to the occasion and put on a great performance. I think we were all a little bit shocked to be in the position we were [at half-time]. Sarina said to keep doing what we were doing and don't concede goals and we did that tonight."

– Beth Mead

"We will definitely enjoy tonight because it was amazing. It was an incredible performance and to do it in front of this crowd in the European Championships was amazing."

– Ellen White

NORTHERN IRELAND v ENGLAND

GROUP A - MATCHDAY 3

St Mary's Stadium

15 July 2022

PRE-MATCH BUILD-UP:

"We want to do well every game, we want to show everyone how good we can play. Yes, we know we've qualified already for the next stage, but there's going to be lots of people watching us: there's going to be 30,000 people in the stadium and we want to play a good game. We want to win and we don't want to concede any goals.

"I'm very proud of the two performances so far. We know the opening match was a hard one. It's also the situation, the first game in England so I think that was a really good performance, a good win and Wednesday was really good too. I think Norway didn't have a good day which made the score so high and we know for the next games it's going to be harder again."

– Sarina Wiegman

"It's been an amazing start [to the tournament]. I think in each and every one of the last three major tournaments we've been in, we've started really well, so that's the focus: to continue the start we've had. And, we've got to keep our feet on the ground because there are other tests ahead."

– Nikita Parris

FIVE-STAR ENGLAND ARE TOP-CLASS FINISHERS

They may have already guaranteed top spot in the group but for Sarina Wiegman, consistency is everything.

For the third game running the England coach named the same team, not that she was able to witness the match in person as she stayed away from the stadium, having tested positive for COVID, with assistant Arjan Veurink leading from the touchline instead.

If the thought process behind the team selection was to ensure the host nation kept up a high level of performance, then it certainly worked as over 30,000 people at the St Mary's Stadium watched England score five more goals to reach 14 in the group stage – more than any other side in EURO history.

High-quality finishing was the story of the game and it was Fran Kirby who provided the first example to score her first goal of the tournament.

Northern Ireland held out until the 40th minute when Kirby placed a wonderful shot into the top-right corner from just outside the box. It was a finish worthy of the biggest stage.

A few minutes later England had their second as Beth Mead continued her superb goalscoring form by placing a lovely left-footed strike just inside the post.

Alessia Russo came off the bench at half-time and didn't take long to find her range. Three minutes after the break she expertly guided a header past Jacqueline Burns following a deft cross from Mead.

Russo had her second five minutes later. Fellow substitute Ella Toone played a through-ball, and the striker span onto the pass and slotted past Burns.

The scoring was completed when the unfortunate Kelsie Burrows diverted a cross over her own 'keeper with 15 minutes remaining.

Northern Ireland could be proud of their first appearance at a UEFA Women's EURO, but for England the knock-out phase beckoned.

NORTHERN IRELAND
18

"WE WANTED TO DO THE FANS PROUD AND ENJOY THE MOMENT. EVERY TIME THEY SHOW UP LIVE IN THE STADIUM IT'S A MASSIVE HELP."

– Rachel Daly

Beth Mead was at it again, scoring a great goal against Northern Ireland in a game when Fran Kirby and Alessia Russo got in on the scoring act too with some high-quality finishes

Northern Ireland 0
England 5

Kirby 41
Mead 45
Russo 48, 53
Burrows 76 (og)

Northern Ireland: Burns, McKenna, Nelson (Hutton 87), McFadden, Vance, L Rafferty (Burrows 66), Callaghan (c) (Wilson 87), Furness (Caldwell 80), Holloway (Magee 66), Wade, K McGuinness.

England: Earps, Bronze (Carter 74), Bright (Greenwood 46), Williamson (c), Daly, Stanway (Toone 46), Walsh, Kirby, Mead, Hemp (Kelly 60), White (Russo 46).

UEFA Player of the Match: Alessia Russo

23
14
7

POST-MATCH:

"For the first 30 minutes, to be fair to Northern Ireland, they did well — we didn't use the right spaces to play in and that's one of the things we tried to put some attention on. We did really well in the first part of the second half. Sometimes, when opponents are defending in a low block, it is really difficult.

"We keep on going with a good game plan. We try to develop game by game and that's what we've done pretty well so far. Hopefully we can continue that journey."

– Arjan Veurink, England assistant head coach

"It's great to give the fans something to celebrate. We love to be ruthless, we love to score goals and, hopefully, there is more of that to come. It's maybe something we've lacked in the past, but at this tournament we're really growing."

– Alessia Russo

"I've been wanting to get a goal through the tournament and have been getting myself in good positions but it hasn't come off for me. Luckily, today I was in the right place and I got good contact on the ball and it was one of those you're watching to see if it goes in — so when it did I was just really happy to open my account."

– Fran Kirby

OUR YEAR
8

DEFENDER

LEAH WILLIAMSON

Leah Williamson played a heroic captain's role in her country's summer European Championship success. The centre-half played every single minute of the tournament. It can be no coincidence that with Williamson marshalling the backline, England kept four clean sheets from their six European Championship matches.

And the EURO 2022 final win over Germany saw an elated Williamson holding aloft the trophy in front of a jubilant Wembley home crowd.

The Milton Keynes-born defender started her footballing journey back in 2006, when she signed for Arsenal at the age of nine. Since joining the Gunners, Williamson has become one of the club's biggest youth team success stories.

Having featured plenty of times at age grade level, 2014 saw Williamson break into the Arsenal first team. At just 17 years old, she made her senior team debut in the Champions League when she came on late in the second half against Birmingham City, replacing England legend Rachel Yankey.

While the Gunners went on to lose the game 2-0, it marked another step in Williamson's journey to England captain.

Her debut campaign saw Williamson make 25 appearances in all competitions, as she also went on to claim the FA Women's Super League Cup Player of the Year.

And following her strong showings during the 2014-15 WSL campaign, Williamson

was further recognised for her Arsenal performances when she was named PFA Young Women's Player of the Year.

She was also named England Women's Youth Player for 2014 too. Since her breakthrough campaign back in 2014, Williamson has gone on to become one of Arsenal's most important players.

The die-hard Arsenal fan was instrumental in helping the Gunners secure multiple domestic titles, which include the 2015 and 2017 FA WSL Cups, the 2015 FA Women's Cup and the 2017-18 FA WSL title.

While she was called up to the England senior squad in November 2017, Williamson had to wait until the summer of 2018 to make her debut.

In June 2018, Williamson came off the bench against Russia to earn her first England cap. She also scored her first England goal the following year, in November 2019, with a late winner over the Czech Republic, and has gone on to make many more appearances for England since.

Williamson has also starred at every age grade level for England from the Under-15s through to the senior side.

She captained her country at the Under-17 Women's European Championship in

'IT CAN BE NO COINCIDENCE THAT WITH WILLIAMSON MARSHALLING THE BACKLINE, ENGLAND KEPT FOUR CLEAN SHEETS FROM THEIR SIX MATCHES'

2013, and also proudly represented England at the Women's Under-20 World Cup in 2014.

In 2021, Williamson was named England captain for a FIFA World Cup qualifier by Sarina Wiegman, a game they went on to win 8-0.

Then in April 2022, she was appointed captain on a permanent basis by Wiegman for the European Championship which England went on to win at a sun soaked Wembley.

STATS

DOB: 29/03/1997	England debut: 08/06/2018 v Russia
Club: Arsenal	UEFA EURO 2022 apps: 6
Position: Defender	UEFA EURO 2022 goals: 0

15

DEFENDER

DEMI STOKES

Demi Stokes may not have featured on the pitch during England's victorious European Championship campaign but the value she added off the field was equally important as that provided by those who did. As a more experienced player among a young squad, West Midlands-born Stokes provided a fascinating insight into the role of a squad member by explaining: "For those that are not playing, it is about pushing your team-mates and how you can help them."

Such a mentality is only to be expected from someone who conducts herself with the utmost professionalism off the field and has won well over half-a-century of caps for England. Alongside Lucy Bronze, Stokes was the only other member of the Lionesses camp to have enjoyed European success previously, in the 2009 UEFA Women's Under-19 Championship.

While not towering in stature, Stokes is without doubt one of the strongest characters within Sarina Wiegman's squad. Her first senior appearance at an international tournament came in 2017, where she was part of a squad that reached the semi-final, before also featuring at the 2019 World Cup in France. Yet, her path to becoming a European champion differs from the majority of her fellow squad members.

Having moved to the North-East at a young age, Stokes' all-female side competed in a male league, something she credits with giving her the physical attributes to make the

very top. Having graduated through Sunderland's youth system, Stokes helped the club win the 2008-09 FA Women's Premier League Northern Division and reach the 2009 Women's FA Cup final alongside future England stars Bronze and Jordan Nobbs.

Two years later she made the bold decision to accept a four-year scholarship to the University of South Florida. While missing the inaugural seasons of the WSL, Stokes experienced a professional lifestyle by training every day and playing twice a week. In addition to featuring regularly for her college, Stokes made 13 appearances for Vancouver Whitecaps in the North American W-League.

Later than most within the current set-up, she would finally make her WSL debut in 2015 after agreeing a three-year deal with Manchester City. A naturally left-sided full-back with pace and impressive close control, Stokes was part of a City defence that conceded just four goals across the 2016 campaign and were crowned champions without losing a single match.

Regarded as an integral part of City's recent success due to her unwavering

'STOKES PROVIDED A FASCINATING INSIGHT INTO THE ROLE OF THE SQUAD PLAYER BY EXPLAINING: "FOR THOSE THAT ARE NOT PLAYING IT IS ABOUT PUSHING YOUR TEAM-MATES AND HOW YOU CAN HELP THEM"'

consistency, Stokes is the club's fourth-highest appearance maker at the time of writing, winning three FA Cups and three League Cups in addition to the aforementioned WSL title at the club. In both 2018 and 2019, she was named in the PFA WSL Team of the Year and has undoubtedly become one of the division's best left-backs.

2022 is certainly a year Stokes will never forget. In the build-up to EURO 2022 she became a mother after partner Katie gave birth to their son Harlen, something Stokes admitted gave her "extra motivation" to perform.

STATS

DOB: 12/12/1991	England debut: 17/01/2014 v Norway
Club: Manchester City	UEFA EURO 2022 apps: 0
Position: Defender	UEFA EURO 2022 goals: 0

20

MIDFIELDER

ELLA TOONE

Tyldesley-born forward Ella Toone is one of England's finest young talents.

Toone was vital to England's European Championship success this summer, including scoring the opening goal in the final against Germany.

Toone started off her footballing journey at Manchester United in their youth ranks before moving to Blackburn Rovers in 2013 where she impressed.

Toone's performances for Rovers earned a move to Manchester City in 2016 but her minutes on the pitch soon became limited. Such was the class of City's squad at the time, Toone played a peripheral role.

In 2018, Toone opted to move back to Manchester United upon the formation of their professional women's team and it was a decision that saw her thrive.

In her debut campaign, Toone bagged 14 goals in 20 appearances as United cruised to the FA Women's Championship title which saw them lose just one league game.

While she did not score as many as she would have liked the following season in the FA Women's Super League, Toone did manage to produce an incredible five-goal performance against Leicester City in the FA Women's League Cup.

The 2020-21 campaign saw Toone return to her goalscoring best, finishing as United's top goal scorer with 10 goals in all competitions. Then last term, she helped United to their third consecutive fourth-place WSL finish.

In terms of her international career, Toone has featured at age grade for England, playing for the Under-17s, Under-19s and Under-21s. She was part of the Under-17s side that appeared at the 2016 FIFA Under-17 World Cup in Jordan.

Had she not picked up an injury in the summer of 2018, she would almost certainly have played a part in England's Under-20 World Cup campaign in France, which saw the Young Lionesses finish third.

Her performances during the 2020-21 season for United saw her earn her first call-up to the senior national team too, with Toone making her England debut against Northern Ireland in February 2021.

She was also part of Great Britain's Tokyo 2020 Olympic squad with Toone making a stoppage-time appearance for Team GB in their opening group stage 2-0 win over Chile.

Since her international debut, Toone has gone on to become one of Wiegman's most reliable players.

Her late equaliser against Spain in the quarter-final of EURO 2022 sparked a magical comeback with Georgia Stanway scoring the winner in extra-time.

To date, she has bagged more than a goal per game for England and looks set to be an international star for years to come.

'SINCE HER INTERNATIONAL DEBUT, TOONE HAS GONE ON TO BECOME ONE OF WIEGMAN'S MOST RELIABLE PLAYERS. HER LATE EQUALISER AGAINST SPAIN SPARKED A MAGICAL COMEBACK'

STATS

DOB: 02/09/1999	England debut: 23/02/2021 v Northern Ireland
Club: Manchester United	UEFA EURO 2022 apps: 6
Position: Midfielder	UEFA EURO 2022 goals: 2

OUR YEAR
11

FORWARD

LAUREN HEMP

It was Lauren Hemp's outswinging corner that led to England's EURO-winning goal in front of a record-breaking 87,192 crowd at Wembley. At just 22, her contribution to her national team had already been monumental and it will be little surprise if Hemp continues to create more lasting memories.

The Norfolk-born attacker netted the second goal in England's 8-0 win against Norway this summer, adding to the ever-growing list of achievements during her international career thus far.

Having debuted for England in 2019, Hemp scored four goals in one match as her side registered a 20–0 win against Latvia, making national history in the process. Indicative of Hemp's talent, UEFA named her as one of Europe's ten most promising young players in 2020.

Often utilised on the left-hand side of an attacking unit, Hemp is prolific in both creating chances and converting them, while she also carries electrifying pace. Kelly Smith, one of England's greatest players, has described Hemp as one of the few players that "get me off my seat" due to her "lethal" nature of play.

Her journey to stardom would begin with taking the bold decision to leave childhood club Norwich City at just 16 to join Bristol City.

In a glimpse of the success that would follow, Hemp scored on her senior debut for

the Vixens in 2016 before being named as PFA Women's Young Player of the Year two years later, after finding the net on seven occasions across the WSL campaign.

In the summer of 2018, Hemp signed for Manchester City and had already captained England at the UEFA Women's Under-17 Championship, in addition to featuring at the 2018 FIFA Under-20 Women's World Cup.

Hemp has quickly amassed 30 goals for City and scored in their 2018 3-0 FA Cup final win against West Ham United at Wembley. Despite enjoying the glory of lifting the country's first European title, Hemp would suffer heartbreak at the national stadium earlier in the summer when her 42nd-minute strike was not enough to defeat Chelsea in the FA Cup final. She made her 100th appearance for City that April.

Further history would be made when Hemp became the first player to win four awards in the same category when she was named PFA Women's Young Player of the Year for the fourth time. She was nominated for the main award too, as well as securing a spot on the WSL Team of The Year.

Olympic recognition was forthcoming in 2021 when Hemp was selected as the

'INDICATIVE OF HEMP'S TALENT, UEFA NAMED HER AS ONE OF EUROPE'S 10 MOST PROMISING PLAYERS IN 2020'

youngest footballer for Team GB in the Tokyo Olympics. She made a notable impact in the competition by assisting Ellen White to score her side's first goal of the competition against Chile and registered another assist in the 4-3 quarter-final defeat to Australia.

Hemp's heroic status was further set into stone when she was awarded the Freedom of the Town on return to her hometown of North Walsham in Norfolk after the glorious summer of 2022. With streets packed out, Hemp's achievements had "brought the whole community together" according to the local MP. She featured in every one of England's tournament matches, providing a constant source of attacking output with an average of two shots per game.

STATS

DOB: 07/08/2000	England debut: 08/10/2019 v Portugal
Club: Manchester City	UEFA EURO 2022 apps: 6
Position: Forward	UEFA EURO 2022 goals: 1

13

GOALKEEPER

HANNAH HAMPTON

When Hannah Hampton was told she would never be able to play sport growing up because of problems with her vision, being part of England's first-ever European Championship triumph must have seemed little more than a pipe dream. Nevertheless, she has managed to defy medical opinion amid a host of other hurdles, something the Birmingham-born shot-stopper can look back on with immense pride.

Her journey to European glory has not been a straightforward one. Diagnosed with a depth perception condition, Hampton has explained that she "can't judge any distances" and was born with a squint, leaving her severely cross-eyed. She has previously admitted: "I don't get how I'm a goalkeeper, I don't understand." Hampton wears contact lenses due to having one short-sighted eye and one long-sighted and occasionally has to call on the physios for help when lenses drop out during matches.

If having to undergo several operations in her junior years was not enough for Hampton to contend with, she moved far from home aged just five when her family emigrated from the Midlands to a town called Alcossebre on the east coast of Spain. With her parents becoming teachers at a local school, it was there where she found her love and talent for football.

Playing as a striker initially, Hampton was encouraged by former Villarreal and

Argentina defender Fabio Fuentes to trial with the club and would thrive on playing with locals despite attending in her West Bromwich Albion kit. She would even end up as the top goalscorer in consecutive seasons.

Upon her return to England, the Villarreal striker would soon transition into a Stoke City goalkeeper, though she would suffer "many nosebleeds" and "a lot of broken fingers," in the process. A move to Birmingham City's Centre of Excellence in 2016 would follow and Hampton made a senior debut for the Blues a year later, eventually becoming a WSL regular throughout the 2018-19 campaign, making headlines as part of a defence that conceded a joint-third low 17 league goals. She was subsequently named the club's Young Player of the Season.

International recognition would follow for Hampton after progressing through respective England age groups. She kept consecutive clean sheets in her two appearances at the 2019 UEFA Women's Under-19 Championship and received her first under-21 call-up in the same year.

In 2021, Hampton followed Birmingham boss Carla Ward to second city rivals Aston Villa. Ward, while admitting she may perhaps be biased, believes Hampton is the best goalkeeper in the country. She then made her senior England debut in the 0-0 Arnold Clark Cup draw against Spain.

'SHE HAS MANAGED TO DEFY MEDICAL OPINION AMID A HOST OF OTHER HURDLES, SOMETHING THE BIRMINGHAM-BORN SHOT-STOPPER CAN LOOK BACK ON WITH IMMENSE PRIDE'

Off the field, Hampton's attributes are almost as impressive as those she has demonstrated on it. She can speak fluent Spanish and is able to communicate effectively in French. Remarkably, Hampton also learned sign language in order to communicate with her cousin. She has become an ambassador for Birmingham Children's Hospital and intends to visit young people in the same wards she was once treated on by using her surreal story to "change mindsets."

Along with Mary Earps and Ellie Roebuck, Hampton is always ready to be called upon when her country needs her. Not bad for somebody who had 'no chance' of playing sport.

STATS

DOB: 16/10/2000	England debut: 20/02/2022 v Spain
Club: Aston Villa	UEFA EURO 2022 apps: 0
Position: Goalkeeper	UEFA EURO 2022 clean sheets: 0

OUR YEAR
2

DEFENDER

LUCY BRONZE

Widely recognised as one of the greatest-ever female footballers, Lucy Bronze can now say she has the international silverware to match both her domestic and individual accolades. A major part of the England team that finished fourth in the 2019 World Cup, Bronze helped her team go all the way this year by netting the second goal in the semi-final win over Sweden. Bronze also won the ball from the corner that led to Chloe Kelly's historic winner against Germany in the final.

After becoming the first English player to win the UEFA Women's Player of the Year award and winning Best FIFA Women's Player in 2020, Bronze has grown accustomed to success throughout her career but admitted that she would have swapped all her individual honours to secure her country's first major trophy.

Her path to becoming a global superstar is a fascinating one, spanning across Sunderland, America, Liverpool, Lyon, Manchester and now Barcelona.

Born to a Portuguese father and an English mother in Berwick-upon-Tweed, Bronze was encouraged to pursue a tennis career as opposed to one in football.

Bronze debuted for England in 2013 and travelled to the European Championship that summer. A first England goal followed a year later as she featured in the first England women's match at Wembley Stadium.

Strong and athletic, Bronze starred at the 2015 World Cup in Canada, scoring in

knock-out wins against Norway and the hosts, and was eventually shortlisted for the Golden Ball.

Such is her talent, Bronze was promoted to Sunderland's senior team when she turned 16 in 2007 and within the next two years would help the club win promotion and feature in her first-ever FA Cup final. She joined Everton in 2010 to participate in the inaugural WSL campaign and UEFA Women's Champions League, before joining rivals Liverpool two years later, where her first taste of WSL glory would be forthcoming in 2013 and 2014.

Having been crowned PFA Women's Players' Player of the Year in 2014, Bronze signed for Manchester City, where her second season with the club coincided with one of the most remarkable WSL campaigns to date. She would be an influential part of an unbeaten City team that only conceded four goals on their way to the title.

The next step was a move abroad to Olympique Lyonnais, where Bronze would help establish the team as Europe's best. Her first season saw a 12th straight league title and, notably, a Champions League win for the first time in her career. She was shortlisted for the inaugural Women's Ballon d'Or award in 2018 as Lyon retained their league and Champions League titles while also regaining the Coupe de France. Bronze was listed

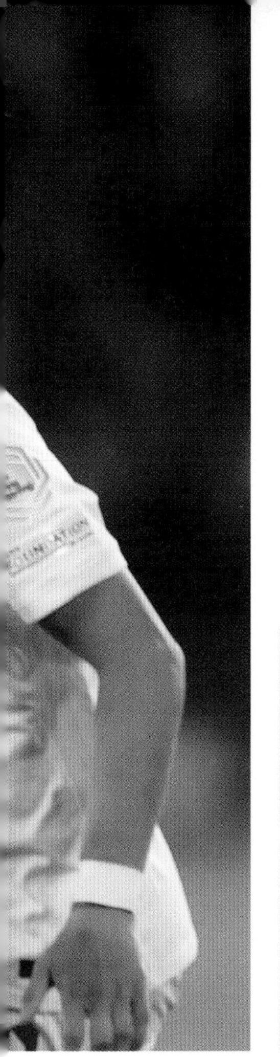

'AFTER BECOMING THE FIRST ENGLISH PLAYER TO WIN THE UEFA WOMEN'S PLAYER OF THE YEAR AWARD AND WINNING BEST FIFA WOMEN'S PLAYER IN 2020, BRONZE HAS GROWN ACCUMSTOMED TO SUCCESS'

as runner-up in the Ballon d'Or in 2019 as Lyon recorded back-to-back trebles in 2020 before Bronze brought the curtain down on a trophy-laden spell in France for a second spell with Manchester City. Prior to her long-awaited international success Bronze signed for Barcelona in June.

Unbeknown to many at the time, Bronze recently revealed that a knee operation prior to the Olympics meant she played through the EURO in pain, meaning she does "not feel like I did a couple of years ago." Typical of Bronze, it did not show in her performances where she featured in every match and also registered two assists, including one for eventual top scorer Beth Mead against Sweden. Never one to rest on her laurels, Bronze has set her sights on following the EURO 2022 win by lifting the 2023 World Cup.

STATS

DOB: 28/10/1991	England debut: 26/06/13 v Japan
Club: Barcelona	UEFA EURO 2022 apps: 6
Position: Defender	UEFA EURO 2022 goals: 1

23

FORWARD

ALESSIA RUSSO

While Chloe Kelly's 110th-minute winner against Germany in the EURO 2022 final might have been England's most important goal, there's no doubt Alessia Russo's audacious backheel against Sweden in the semi-final was their best.

Coming off the bench in the second half, Russo saw her initial shot blocked by Sweden shot stopper Hedvig Lindahl. With the ball running wide and Russo seemingly running out of space, it looked as though the Manchester United forward had fluffed her lines.

However, to the delight of the 28,624 spectators inside Bramall Lane, Russo produced a magical back-heeled strike which slipped between Lindahl's legs to the joy of England supporters.

It was a goal that summed up Russo's game – a dynamic forward who has plenty more to offer on the international stage.

The Maidstone-born striker finished EURO 2022 with four goals to her name, with only team-mate Beth Mead and Germany's Alexandra Popp scoring more with six each.

Russo began her footballing journey at Charlton Athletic before later joining Chelsea where she made her senior debut in the FA Women's Super League Cup back in 2016 against London Bees.

A move to Brighton & Hove Albion a year later followed before Russo opted to move

stateside to play college 'soccer' for the North Carolina Tar Heels of the University of North Carolina.

Russo thrived out in America, plying her trade in the NCAA's Atlantic Coast Conference. 2017 saw the Tar Heels win the ACC Women's Soccer Tournament with Russo being named Most Valuable Player.

While a broken leg curtailed her 2018 season, Russo bounced back in 2019 as the Tar Heels reclaimed their ACC championship title. And after bagging the winning goal in the ACC final against Virginia in extra time, Russo was once again named the tournament's MVP.

The following year saw Russo opt to leave America to join Manchester United, where she enjoyed a promising return to the English domestic game. However, her season was curtailed in devastating fashion in November, after she suffered a hamstring injury in training.

Russo bounced back last term by scoring 11 goals in all competitions for the Red Devils, helping them to a fourth-place finish in the WSL.

On the international front, Russo has represented every age group for England. She

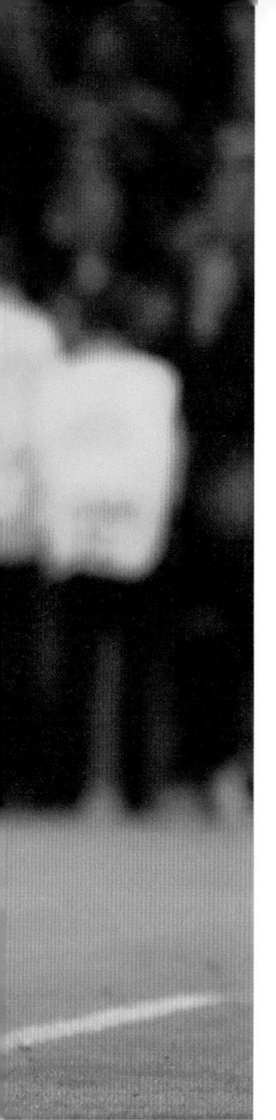

'RUSSO PRODUCED A MAGICAL BACK-HEELED STRIKE. IT WAS A GOAL THAT SUMMED UP HER GAME – A DYNAMIC FORWARD WHO AT 23 YEARS OLD HAS PLENTY MORE TO OFFER'

was part of the England Under-20s side that won bronze at the 2018 Under-20 FIFA Women's World Cup.

She made her England debut back in March 2020 in the SheBelieves Cup against Spain. In November 2021, Russo bagged her first international goals, a hat-trick, in England's record-breaking 20-0 win over Latvia. The hat-trick took her just 11 minutes to score, which was the fastest by any England player in history.

While she made all six of her appearances at EURO 2022 off the bench, Ellen White's recent retirement has left a space upfront for England. Russo could be the player to fill that void.

STATS

DOB: 08/02/1999	England debut: 11/03/2020 v Spain
Club: Manchester United	UEFA EURO 2022 apps: 6
Position: Forward	UEFA EURO 2022 goals: 4

OUR YEAR
18

FORWARD

CHLOE KELLY

Chloe Kelly has forever written herself into English football history as the scorer of the goal that sealed a first-ever European Championship title for her country. At just 24 years old, Kelly's status as a national hero and inspiration to many was already secured forever. The iconic image of the forward swinging her shirt above her head in pandemonium at Wembley will live long in the memory.

However, Kelly's thoughts could not have been further away from scoring a European Championship-winning goal not so long ago. Simply featuring in Sarina Wiegman's squad for the tournament was a success for the London-born forward.

In May 2021, Kelly suffered an anterior cruciate ligament injury when playing for Manchester City in the WSL. The injury, one of the most severe to a footballer, kept her out of action for just under 11 months and left Kelly with only six weeks to convince Wiegman she was worthy of a place in the squad.

Kelly admitted she "couldn't actually face watching" the Tokyo Olympics last year when she remained sidelined. Nevertheless, her determination to make up for lost time and dispel the negativity surrounding ACL injuries saw Kelly return to action in April and subsequently secure a place in the squad.

Such was the achievement her return to fitness represented, England and former Manchester City team-mate Lucy Bronze revealed, "Chloe was the first one I wanted

to see to congratulate" when being named in the squad, having "stood by her side and watched her climb that mountain" after both players endured time on the sidelines.

Those who have kept a keen eye on Kelly's domestic progress would not have been shocked to see her goalscoring instinct on show at Wembley when the ball ricocheted off Bronze before being turned past Germany goalkeeper Merle Frohms in the final.

Having graduated from Arsenal's academy and debuted for the club in 2015, Kelly discovered her goalscoring touch during a loan spell with Everton in 2016. She would return to Merseyside again on loan upon promotion in 2017 and turned her move into a permanent one a year later.

Having undergone ankle surgery in 2019, Kelly embarked on a prolific spell in front of goal. She netted nine times in 12 appearances for the Toffees during the 2019-20 campaign, finishing the season as her club's top scorer and the WSL's fourth-highest. She made headlines when scoring two superb long-range goals in one game, seeing her named September's WSL Player of the Month. Her efforts saw Kelly named in the PFA WSL Team of the Year, prior to leaving for City in 2020.

'THOSE THAT HAVE KEPT A KEEN EYE ON KELLY'S PROGRESS WOULD NOT HAVE BEEN SHOCKED TO SEE HER GOALSCORING INSTINCT ON SHOW AT WEMBLEY'

Kelly's celebration after the deciding action of the EURO 2022 final was certainly befitting of the moment she made history. Her post-match interview, which totalled roughly 23 words before she embarked on joining in with the chorus of Sweet Caroline, cannot be forgotten either. It was poignant that the childhood QPR supporter would relive her very own "Bobby Zamora moment," as she turned her status into that of a household name.

STATS

DOB: 15/01/1998	England debut: 08/11/2018 v Austria
Club: Manchester City	UEFA EURO 2022 apps: 6
Position: Forward	UEFA EURO 2022 goals: 1

DEFENDER

ALEX GREENWOOD

Another member of England's faultless defensive unit, Alex Greenwood can possibly feel unfortunate not to have played a greater role in the victorious EURO 2022 campaign. Her multitude of caps and the long list of well-established clubs she has represented are evidence of Greenwood's quality.

Capable of dominating opposition attackers as either a left full-back or centre-back, Greenwood has also developed a reputation as a high-quality set-piece taker. She was entrusted by Sarina Wiegman to feature in vital extra-time periods against Spain and Germany.

Greenwood was the youngest member of England's squad at the 2015 FIFA Women's World Cup and started in her team's third-place play-off win over Germany. The Liverpool-born star was also a crucial part of the side that reached the semi-final of EURO 2017, prior to coming away with a winner's medal five years later. Adding to her international pedigree, Greenwood was a key figure of the squad that reached the semi-final of the 2019 World Cup in France.

She has been involved in the game since the age of eight when Greenwood joined Everton. Having progressed through the club's Centre of Excellence, her senior debut arrived in a UEFA Women's Champions League qualification match, before going on to score in the competition only two days later. Greenwood became a regular starter

during the 2011 WSL campaign and her performances the following season were to such a high standard that she was named FA Young Player of the Year.

Upon the Toffees' relegation in 2014, Greenwood signed for Notts County but returned to Merseyside two years later by signing for the team she supported as a child, Liverpool. The 29-year-old made headlines back in 2018 when she captained Manchester United's women's team during their first-ever season, helping the club win promotion to the WSL at the first time of asking under former England star Casey Stoney's stewardship.

In 2019, however, a transfer to Olympique Lyonnais beckoned for Greenwood, where she linked up with England team-mates Lucy Bronze and Nikita Parris. Throughout her single season in France, Greenwood won every trophy on offer as the club sealed their fourth consecutive Champions League crown on top of domestic honours.

Greenwood returned to England in 2020 by signing a three-year deal with Manchester City, a move Bronze would also make that summer. She has been described as one of the team's unsung heroes by City team-mates, with superb distribution and an excellent passing range, complemented by a willingness to put her body on the line for the cause.

Greenwood has admirably captained the club on several occasions in the absence of

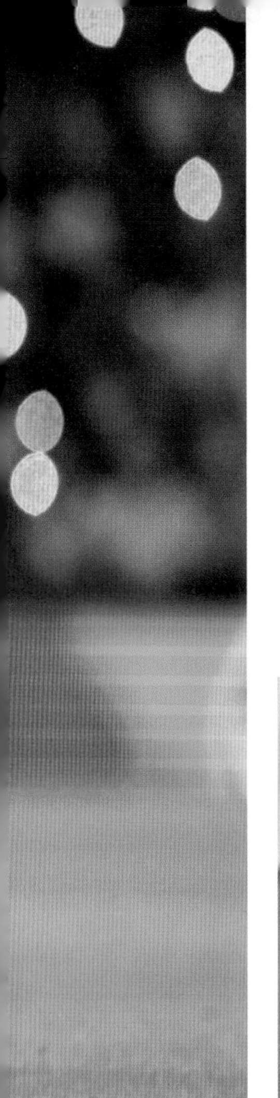

'CAPABLE OF DOMINATING OPPOSITION ATTACKERS AS EITHER A LEFT-BACK OR CENTRE-BACK, GREENWOOD HAS ALSO DEVELOPED A REPUTATION AS A HIGH-QUALITY SET-PIECE TAKER'

Steph Houghton and Ellen White. She won the Women's FA Cup final for the first time in 2020 and lifted the League Cup earlier this year, eventually earning a spot in the PFA WSL 2021-22 Team of the Year. Interestingly, Greenwood has played for both major teams in Liverpool and Manchester, something only former England international Peter Beardsley can also claim to have done.

In each of her five substitute appearances across the summer, Greenwood added priceless experience and know-how to proceedings to help bring football home.

STATS

DOB: 07/09/1993	England debut: 05/03/2014 v Italy
Club: Manchester City	UEFA EURO 2022 apps: 5
Position: Defender	UEFA EURO 2022 goals: 0

14

MIDFIELDER

FRAN KIRBY

Fran Kirby's physical stature may be slight but she is a titan of the women's game and one of the finest footballers England has ever produced.

At the heart of the highest-ever scoring EURO team in a creative midfield role, Kirby almost directly contributed to a goal every game and netted in the semi-final win over Sweden to cap off a magnificent display. Kirby's journey to becoming an international superstar has been a rollercoaster ride though, encountering setbacks that many would struggle to overcome.

Kirby was showing a footballer's instinct from the age of just three and joined her hometown team, Reading, at the age of seven. She progressed through the Royals' youth system and debuted for the club aged 16 before her mother's sudden passing three years earlier took its toll and saw Kirby turn her back on the sport as she battled depression.

Nonetheless, her comeback with Sunday League side Reading Town Ladies convinced Kirby to return to competitive action. She would score 32 goals in the 2012-13 season, prior to netting 24 times, including three hat-tricks, upon the club's promotion to the second tier a year later.

Having become Reading's first women's player to receive a professional contract and been named the inaugural WSL2 Players' Player of the Year, Kirby received international

recognition when becoming the first WSL2 player to be called up to the senior England squad.

Another stellar campaign followed for Kirby, which saw her named in the England squad for the 2015 FIFA Women's World Cup in Canada, where she scored her side's first goal in a 2-1 win against Mexico and was dubbed 'mini Messi.'

Off the back of the World Cup, Kirby earned a move to Chelsea for what was reported to be a British record transfer fee at the time.

In October 2015, she scored Chelsea's first UEFA Women's Champions League goal. Kirby was named the PFA Women's Players' Player of the Year and the Football Writers' Women's Footballer of the Year for the 2017-18 season after netting 22 goals on the way to winning the WSL title.

In February 2020, a further stumbling block was presented to Kirby when she was diagnosed with pericarditis, a condition affecting the fluid-filled sac around the heart that had sidelined her from November. Despite warnings from doctors, Kirby continued to defy odds and returned to fitness in August.

Courtesy of 16 goals and 11 assists, Kirby claimed the Football Writers' Women's

'KIRBY'S JOURNEY TO BECOMING AN INTERNATIONAL SUPERSTAR HAS BEEN A ROLLERCOASTER RIDE, ENCOUNTERING SETBACKS THAT MANY WOULD STRUGGLE TO OVERCOME'

Footballer of the Year in 2021, with the Blues becoming the first English women's club to win the domestic quadruple.

Incredibly, a fatigue problem had appeared to jeopardise Kirby's place at the 2022 European Championship. She even confessed that she "didn't even think about being in the squad in February to April time."

Of course, Kirby battled back as she always seems to do, finishing the championship with two goals and three assists. Her strike against Northern Ireland was among the tournament's best and was unlucky not to feature higher in the goal of the tournament standings.

STATS

DOB: 29/06/1993
Club: Chelsea
Position: Midfielder

England debut: 03/08/2014 v Sweden
UEFA EURO 2022 apps: 6
UEFA EURO 2022 goals: 2

OUR YEAR
1

FORWARD

BETH MEAD

There's no question that without Beth Mead, England would not have won the European Championship in 2022. The Whitby-born forward was at the centre of everything England did well.

Mead finished EURO 2022 as the tournament's top goalscorer with six – including a stellar hat-trick in England's 8-0 demolition of Norway – pipping Germany's Alexandra Popp to the award courtesy of her five assists.

Mead's outstanding contribution saw her named UEFA's EURO 2022 Player of the Tournament.

Under Wiegman, who has brought the best out of her, Mead has become one of international football's most dangerous finishers.

Her journey to England stardom began back in 2011 when Mead was turning out for Sunderland, where she nurtured her game during the early stages of her footballing career.

After tearing it up in the lower leagues of the women's game, the future England star was on hand to help the Black Cats achieve promotion to the FA Women's Super League for the 2015 campaign on the final day of the season thanks to a 4-0 win against Millwall.

While the step up to the WSL could have been a concern for some, it was a walk in the park for Mead, who bagged 12 goals in 14 games to finish as the league's top scorer.

Her performances for Sunderland eventually earned her a move to Arsenal in January 2017. The Gunners had tried to prise Mead away from Sunderland back in 2015, but she resisted their overtures so she could finish her Teesside University degree in Sports Development.

Mead performed admirably in her debut season for the Gunners, finishing as their top scorer and their Player of the Season.

While her numbers in front of goal dropped off due to Vivianne Miedema's arrival, Mead became a creative force for Arsenal, helping them to secure the 2018-19 WSL title for the first time since 2012.

Her performances that season earned her a nomination for the FSA's Player of the Year award. She also claimed the WSL's Goal of the Season trophy for her superb long-range strike against Brighton in a 4-0 win which saw the Gunners clinch the title.

Mead was already a world-class talent but under Arsenal boss Jonas Eidevall, the forward has taken her game to the next level.

The 2021-22 season saw the attacking star named Arsenal's Player of the Season

'UNDER WIEGMAN, WHO HAS BROUGHT THE BEST OUT OF HER, MEAD HAS BECOME ONE OF INTERNATIONAL FOOTBALL'S MOST DANGEROUS FINISHERS'

while last term saw her bag 14 goals and register 19 assists in 40 games for the Gunners.

On the international stage, Mead has represented England at every age level from Under-15. 2018 saw her break through into the England senior set-up. She made her international debut against Wales in April, and has gone on to make many appearances for England – and she was named England Women's Player of the Year in 2022.

Those appearances have produced lots of goals already and there is no doubt there are plenty more to come.

STATS

DOB: 09/05/1995	England debut: 06/04/2018 v Wales
Club: Arsenal	UEFA EURO 2022 apps: 6
Position: Forward	UEFA EURO 2022 goals: 6

ENGLAND v SPAIN

QUARTER-FINAL

Brighton & Hove Community Stadium
20 July 2022

PRE-MATCH BUILD-UP:

"It's okay sometimes to not have the ball. We like to have the ball, Spain like to have the ball. That's their style of play. There will be moments when they're tight on the ball and it's not the moment to win it from them. We have to be patient.

"We want to play our best game. If necessary, we know that we can swap and we have players that can really impact the game and that might change the game or give an extra boost. We've showed that in all the other games before, so that's absolutely something that we keep in mind. It's a strength of our team."

– Sarina Wiegman

"Sarina has stayed really well connected with us [while away from the players due to COVID] – her influence on the game has been as usual as possible.

"It's nice to come back somewhere where you've had happy memories [referring to the 8-0 win over Norway]. Hopefully we can pick up where we left off and play a good game.

"I think if you look at the threats that we have and maybe their weaknesses, it's encouraging for us. Definitely, it's a team who are so good at what they do, but there is vulnerability there."

– Leah Williamson

"It's probably one of the strongest squads [we have ever had] in terms of the depth of it, where anyone could make it in the starting XI. All the players play at top teams, have had good seasons, so maybe that's a bit different."

– Lucy Bronze

STANWAY STRIKE SEES ENGLAND PASS THE TEST

This is where the serious business really began and England were handed a mighty task at the quarter-final stage as they faced Spain.

Jorge Vilda's side came into the tournament unbeaten in two years and on a huge upward trajectory.

They were handed two hammer blows on the eve of the tournament as Alexia Putellas and Jennifer Hermoso – a fearsome duo that any international side would love to have – were ruled out with serious knee injuries.

There was still plenty of threat in the Spain camp though and their style of dominating possession had seen them come through a tricky Group D.

England knew they would have to be at their best to reach the semi-finals but they were boosted by the return of Sarina Wiegman from COVID isolation.

She took her place on the touchline for a match where Spain's passing style meant they were likely to see a lot of the ball.

The question was whether England would have enough possession themselves to continue their free-scoring route so far.

Wiegman kept faith with the same starting XI that had served the country so well during their Group A matches and the first half was a tense battle with so much at stake, Spain having six of the seven attempts on goal.

The deadlock was broken nine minutes into the second half and it was Spain who struck first. Substitute Athenea Del Castillo darted into the box from the right, cut the ball back to Esther González and the striker calmly slotted past Mary Earps and the retreating Millie Bright.

This was England's first major taste of adversity during the tournament. They had to find a way to

break down a Spain team that doesn't concede many goals – and that's what they did, though they had to wait until six minutes from time to do so.

When the goal came, it arrived courtesy of two substitutes. Alessia Russo nodded down a cross for the onrushing Ella Toone to smash in from close range.

England's tails were up but a winner couldn't be found until five minutes into extra-time.

Keira Walsh found Georgia Stanway in acres of space in midfield. With no defenders coming to close her down she advanced toward the edge of the box before unleashing a fierce drive that flew past Sandra Paños.

The crowd at the Brighton & Hove Community Stadium erupted and though there were still 25 minutes to go, England negotiated them with few real scares.

The sense of belief was growing stronger. It was time to dream.

Spain made life really tough for England and looked set to go through until Ella Toone slammed in an equaliser, allowing Georgia Stanway to become the match-winner with an outstanding shot from distance

England 2 Spain 1 (aet)

Toone 84 González 54
Stanway 96

England: Earps, Bronze, Bright, Williamson (c), Daly (Greenwood 82), Stanway, Walsh (Scott 116), Kirby (Toone 64), Mead (Kelly 58), Hemp (Parris 116), White (Russo 58).

Spain: Paños, Carmona, León, Paredes (c), Battle, Abelleira (Aleixandri 70), Guijarro, Bonmati, Caldentey (Sarriegi 100), González (Garcia 77), Cardona (Del Castillo 46).

UEFA Player of the Match: Millie Bright

11

ENGLAND 2022

POST-MATCH:

"I think I went crazy! I was so happy! It was so close and I'm so happy that we won. We showed resilience to come from behind. We equalised late and when we scored in extra time we looked a bit fresher, and it meant Spain had to push. I'm sure it was an incredible game for people to watch, and the fans in the stadium were right behind us."

– Sarina Wiegman

POST-MATCH:

"The atmospheres have been incredible. We're embracing the pressure and we're loving every minute. The fans are giving us that momentum, that burst of energy. Everyone has that belief. Tournament football is about momentum, keeping everyone in a good place and nothing changes going into the semis."

– Millie Bright

POST-MATCH:

"That just shows the level that we're at. We get a setback and we come back and do it. We put in a massive shift. Job done and we'll focus on the semis."

– Georgia Stanway

14

ENGLAND v SWEDEN
SEMI-FINAL
Bramall Lane
26 July 2022

PRE-MATCH BUILD-UP:

"Everyone is excited of course. We did some recovery after the last game, we got fresh again and then we started to prepare for the Sweden game. Everyone is so focused and so excited.

"The level of training has been really high again, which is really nice, and I can't wait to play tomorrow.

"It is going to be a really tight game. They have performed really well in the previous years and they have always performed well in the women's game. They are number two in the FIFA ranking so it is going to be a difficult game and totally different to what we faced against Spain because they have a totally different style of play, but we are prepared."

– Sarina Wiegman

"We're so grateful for the fans that support us, whether that's in the stadium or at home and we just want to keep making them proud.

"Hopefully we see everyone's beers flying around and that they're enjoying the game.

"We just want to make everyone proud. That's the main thing: inspiring the next generation.

"Hopefully we can go on and put in another big performance in the semis."

– Ella Toone

"Every game right now is tough and it's the semi-final of a EUROs. Maybe Sweden haven't been at their best but every time we play them, they play pretty good and they're an athletic team with a lot of quality players. So they're not a team we will take lightly and we're looking forward to the challenge."

– Beth Mead

ENGLAND IN DREAMLAND

Semi-finals are meant to be tight, tense affairs with so much at stake that creativity and excitement is stifled as the size of the occasion looms enormously in the minds of the players.

Well, the England and Sweden squads didn't get the memo.

The host nation faced the highest-ranked team at the tournament and with so much to play for, a cautious approach could have been forgiven. What followed was a match that thrilled from the very first minute – and the final scoreline doesn't tell the whole story of a match Sweden played a full part in.

Sarina Wiegman saw no reason to change a winning formula and stuck with the starting line-up that had served her so well as her side faced a country that was appearing in its ninth EURO semi-final.

The capacity crowd at Bramall Lane were revved up for a big occasion but it was Peter Gerhardsson's side that created the first big opportunity inside the first minute. Stina Blackstenius played a lovely through-ball to Sofia Jakobsson who was one-on-one with Mary Earps but the England 'keeper made a fine save with her feet.

It wouldn't be the only time Earps was called into action in the first half, but Beth Mead had a chance at the other end in the first few minutes, though she didn't connect properly with a far-post header.

Sweden would have wanted more reward for their fast start and Earps had to be at her best when Blackstenius scuffed a shot that seemed like it might find the corner but the 'keeper tipped wide. The resulting corner was floated into the middle of the goal, Blackstenius rising highest but her header hit the crossbar and bounced to safety.

Fortunately for England, the game settled down and the next big chance would fall to the woman of the moment, Beth Mead. Lucy Bronze fired in a cross from the right on 34 minutes. Mead's first touch gave her space to swivel and fire an unstoppable strike past Hedvig Lindahl to register her sixth goal of the tournament.

The first goal raised the decibel-level even further in the stadium and the England fans could truly start to believe just three minutes into the second half as Mead returned the compliment to Bronze. The former's corner went over the crowd in the middle

of the box to the full-back who powered a downward header through a ruck of bodies and into the far corner.

Wiegman made her first substitution 12 minutes into the half and Alessia Russo, who replaced Ellen White, made a huge impact.

First, she crossed low to Lauren Hemp, who smashed an effort against the crossbar. Then, just after Blackstenius had again been denied by Earps at the other end, Russo produced a piece of magic.

The striker's initial shot was palmed away by Lindahl but an audacious piece of quick thinking saw Russo backheel an effort past the closing defender and through the 'keeper's legs for the cheekiest of finishes.

There was still time for Fran Kirby to round off a great personal performance by lifting the ball over Lindahl to make it 4-0.

Russo came close to adding further gloss but a resounding victory had Wiegman's buoyant side celebrating wildly on the pitch. England were in the final. The dream was one giant step closer.

It was a semi-final full of incident and excitement and the stand-out moment came when Alessia Russo (left) produced an impudent piece of skill to put England 3-0 up

SWEDEN
26 JULY 2022
2

Booking.co

ENGLAND

England's performance was enough to create hysteria among fans and players alike – and there was even a sneak preview of a Chloe Kelly celebration that would be seen again a few days later

England 4 Sweden 0

Mead 34
Bronze 48
Russo 68
Kirby 76

England: Earps, Bronze, Bright, Williamson (c), Daly (Greenwood 86), Stanway (Scott 86), Walsh, Kirby (Toone 79), Mead (Kelly 86), Hemp, White (Russo 57).

Sweden: Lindahl, Glas, Eriksson, Sembrant (Bennison 76), Ilestedt (Andersson 55), Björn, Asllani (c), Angeldal (Seger 51), Jakobsson (Rytting Kane 51), Blackstenius (Hurtig 76), Rolfö.

UEFA Player of the Match: Beth Mead

9
9

POST-MATCH:

"We'll celebrate now, but before this tournament we had a dream. We've come very far now and no-one can take it away. We played so much better in the second half and it was such a good performance.

"We've shown a couple of times that we're very resilient. They [Sweden] began the game well and they had a good start, but we found a way and we found a way to get out of their pressure. We were so solid and I'm incredibly proud of them."

– Sarina Wiegman

POST-MATCH:

"I missed the first one and we were actually working on cut-backs in training the other day! Once it fell back to me, I thought 'what's the quickest route for me to get this ball in the back of the net?' because I should have scored in the first place, so I just swung a foot at it and luckily it hit the net.

"To score in a semi-final and progress to the final is a huge highlight of my career. I don't normally score backheels and I don't think you'll see one again. I'll take it for now."

– Alessia Russo

"I will speak about one individual, because Mary Earps made a save at a key moment of the game which was an incredible turning point for us. We then went up the other end and scored. That's when you talk about a team, that means a team, that's what the team is about because at two opposite ends of the pitch everybody is making it count.

"That moment deserves a shout out. Everybody today was absolutely incredible and delivered what they needed to deliver, and we go again on Sunday."

– Leah Williamson

"They [Sweden] started the game really well. They opened us up a little bit at times and it was a good time to get the goal. It gave us that extra energy to finish the first half well. The second half, we produced such a dominant display."

– Beth Mead

GERMANY-FRANCE
27 JULY 2022
adidas
15
9
15
adidas

GERMANY EYE ANOTHER TITLE

POPP LEADS CHARGE TO THE FINAL AFTER A TOURNAMENT THAT HAD LIT UP EUROPE

With a place in the semi-final secured, England could prepare for a showpiece occasion – and pay particular attention to the second semi-final between Germany and France to see who they would face at Wembley.

France had a superbly talented side with the ambition to reach the top, while Germany were by far the competition's most successful nation, having won eight of the previous 12 titles.

Pre-match it was a difficult game to call and the 90 minutes ebbed and flowed with both sides having periods of dominance.

As is so often the case, it was Germany who had the knowhow to see them through – and their leading light was once again Alexandra Popp.

The 31-year-old already had four goals at UEFA Women's EURO 2022 before the semi-final, so France couldn't say they didn't know where the threat would come from, but she added two more superb goals in the semi-final.

The Germany captain opened the scoring with a brilliant left-footed volley to convert Svenja Huth's cross but France were level just before the break when Kadidiatou Diani's fierce drive hit the post but rebounded in off the back of goalkeeper Merle Frohms.

The winner from Popp arrived with 14 minutes left on the clock and displayed her hunger to reach the final. France blocked a few efforts on goal before an inviting cross from the right was attacked by Popp, who powerfully headed in.

That brought the German attacker level at the top of the goalscoring charts with England's Beth Mead on six apiece.

Martina Voss-Tecklenburg's side's progress to the final had been almost faultless.

Alexandra Popp was in sensational form at UEFA Women's EURO 2022 and netted both goals in the semi-final against a France team that had beaten the reigning champions, the Netherlands, in the quarter-finals

They negotiated a tough group that contained Denmark, Spain and Finland without conceding a goal and topped the group.

In the quarter-finals they saw off Austria 2-0, Lina Magull grabbing the first goal with Popp sealing victory in the 90th minute, maintaining her record of having scored in every game of the tournament.

The other quarter-finals saw England beat Spain, of course, with Sweden edging past Belgium with an added-time winner, while France needed an extra-time penalty from Ève Périsset to win a heavyweight contest with the Netherlands.

On the back of a group stage which had seen some outstanding individual performances from players from every competing nation in front of enthusiastic supporters, the entertainment on show had been captivating.

No matter who won the final, no-one could argue that it hadn't been an exceptional tournament.

Record numbers of fans had attended matches and been treated to 92 goals in 30 matches.

Would the final live up to expectations and keep up the average of around three goals per game?

GERMANY'S ROUTE TO THE FINAL:

Group B – matchday 1
Brentford Community Stadium
8 July 2022

Germany 4 Denmark 0

Magull 21
Schüller 57
Lattwein 78
Popp 86

Group B – matchday 2
Brentford Community Stadium
12 July 2022

Germany 2 Spain 0

Bühl 3
Popp 37

Group B – matchday 3
Stadium MK
16 July 2022

Finland 0 Germany 3

Kleinherne 40
Popp 48
Anyomi 63

Quarter-final
Brentford Community Stadium
21 July 2022

Germany 2 Austria 0

Magull 25
Popp 90

Semi-final
Stadium MK
27 July 2022

Germany 2 France 1

Popp 40, 76 Frohms 44 (og)

Sweden edged past Belgium in their quarter-final before falling to England, while the ever-dangerous Lina Magull (above left) scored a crucial goal for Germany against Austria

THE RESULTS: MATCH BY MATCH

GROUP A

England 1 Austria 0
Norway 4 N Ireland 1
Austria 2 N Ireland 0
England 8 Norway 0
Austria 1 Norway 0
N Ireland 0 England 5

GROUP B

Spain 4 Finland 1
Germany 4 Denmark 0
Denmark 1 Finland 0
Germany 2 Spain 0
Denmark 0 Spain 1
Finland 0 Germany 3

GROUP C

Portugal 2 Switzerland 2
Netherlands 1 Sweden 1
Sweden 2 Switzerland 1
Netherlands 3 Portugal 2
Sweden 5 Portugal 0
Switzerland 1 Netherlands 4

GROUP D

Belgium 1 Iceland 1
France 5 Italy 1
Italy 1 Iceland 1
France 2 Belgium 1
Italy 0 Belgium 1
Iceland 1 France 1

QUARTER-FINALS

England 2 Spain 1 (aet)

Germany 2 Austria 0

Sweden 1 Belgium 0

France 1 Netherlands 0 (aet)

SEMI-FINALS

England 4 Sweden 0

Germany 2 France 1

FINAL

England v Germany

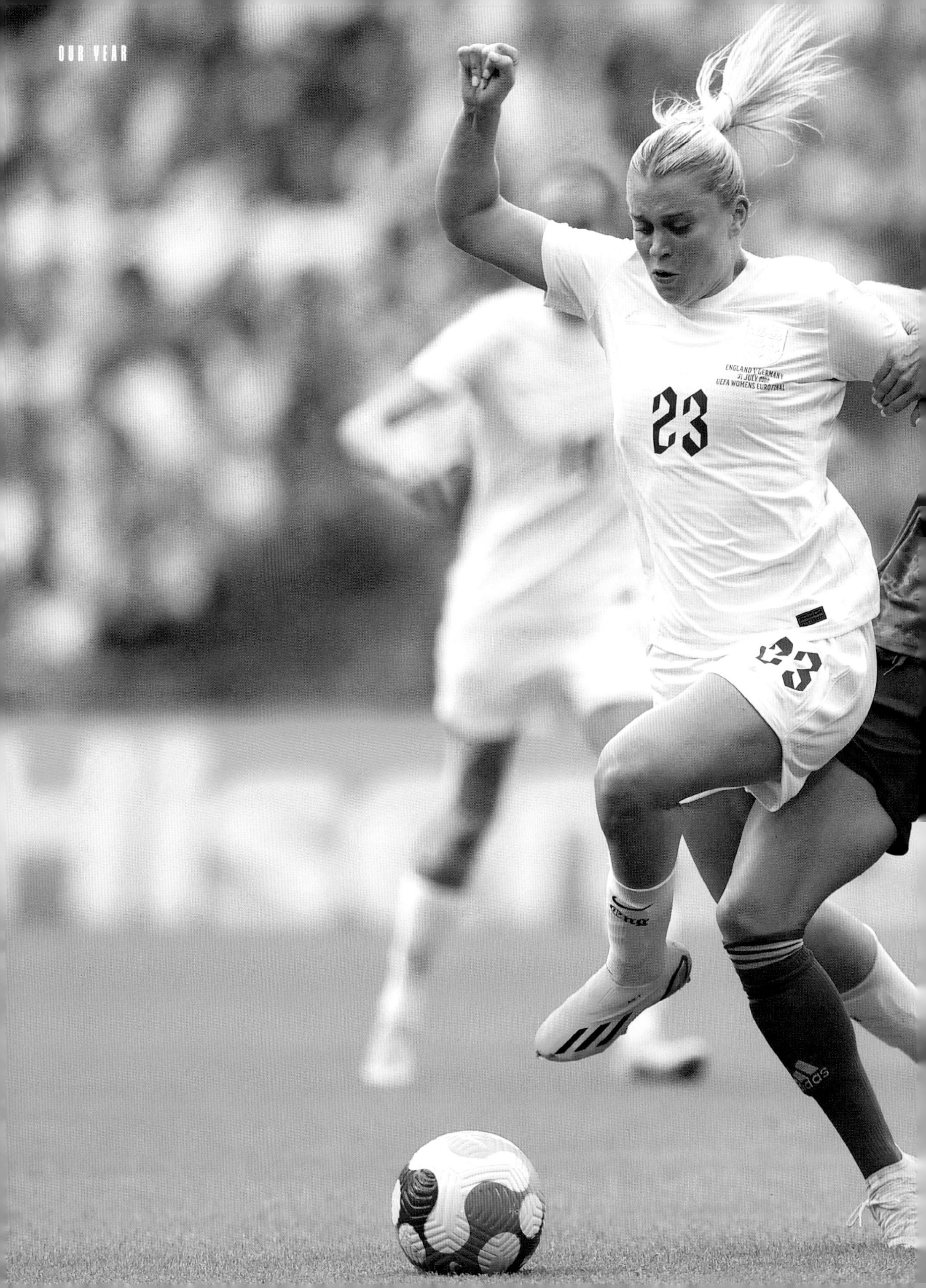
ENGLAND V GERMANY
UEFA WOMENS EUROFINAL
23
23

FINAL

Wembley
31 July 2022

PRE-MATCH BUILD-UP:

"When you reach the final, then you are one of the best teams in the tournament. We have a very good team and we don't fear anyone.
"I think the pressure is on both teams because we both want to win the final and we both have very good squads. I think it is going to be a very tight game. It is going to be exciting.
"We don't feel more or less pressure [than Germany]. It is just a game, it is a very exciting game, with two very good teams who both want to win."

– Sarina Wiegman

"My job is to come here and win that game. That is how I approach every other single game.
"It [continually growing women's football] is definitely not the most important thing but it is something that of course I want. I fight every single day for us as women's footballers. That won't change. I will still do my job as I have every other time. But I do think it is important for that message to come across as well."

–Leah Williamson

"It's unbelievable, the way women's football has grown, especially over the last few weeks. Having packed out stadiums, it's just incredible and to go out on that pitch and hear the crowd roar and then again every single time we score, it just gives us such a boost.
"It's going to be important in the final. Obviously, it's been sold out now for a while and we're so lucky to be there and that has always been the aim, and we're hoping to go that one step further this time. It's going to be an incredible occasion and I can't wait."

– Lauren Hemp

PRE-MATCH BUILD-UP:

"For players like myself, Ellen [White] and Fran [Kirby] who've experienced a lot of semi-final defeats, it's nice to get over those defeats and get over the line and finally get ourselves in the final.

"It's certainly not job done and I think anyone I've spoken to before the tournament knows I was always focused on wanting to win the final.

"Now we've got every chance of doing that. That was a job we came here to do and now we've got ourselves in the best position to do that."

– Lucy Bronze

"The fans have been unbelievable since the very first game at Old Trafford until now. That is what makes it so special, being able to share it with friends, family and the fans.

"Everybody going wild, everybody knows who we are now, so yeah, come on England!"

– Georgia Stanway

READY TO TAKE A PLACE IN FOOTBALL HISTORY

Cometh the hour, cometh the women. After a qualifying stage, three group games and two tough knock-out matches, two of Europe's finest teams remained to battle it out in the final of UEFA Women's EURO 2022 at Wembley.

England had the backing of the majority of the 87,192 people in the crowd and were riding the crest of a wave. Germany were by far the most successful team in European Championship history with eight titles won through the years.

Both sides contained match-winners, but while England had blasted through their semi-final against Sweden 4-0, Germany had edged past a talented France team.

Picking a winner in this encounter would be tough. The match could be decided just as much by bottle as by skill.

Sarina Wiegman had picked the same starting XI for the first five games and put her faith in that selection again.

UEFA Women's EURO 2022
Final
Wembley Stadium
31st July 2022

Ella Toone came off the bench – as she had done in every match of the tournament – to great effect and her delightful lob put England in front at Wembley

Merle Frohms punches clear under pressure from Rachel Daly and Leah Williamson

Germany suffered a hammer blow as top goalscorer Alexandra Popp was ruled out, denying her the chance to score in every game of the tournament.

There was little margin between the teams in a tight first half, by far the best chance going to Germany as a goalmouth scramble resulted in Leah Williamson clearing off the line before Mary Earps pounced on the loose ball.

England's best chance of the opening 45 minutes came when the ball was cut back to Ellen White on the edge of the box but her powerful drive sailed just over the bar.

Germany's first real opportunity of the second half fell to Lina Magull who poked a shot just wide from near the penalty spot.

But just as in previous matches, substitutes would play a huge part for England. On 56 minutes Alessia Russo and Ella Toone came off the bench, as they had done in all of England's matches at the tournament, and the latter broke the deadlock six minutes later.

Keira Walsh advanced with the ball in her own half before threading a delightful long pass into the path of Toone. As Merle Frohms came out to narrow the angle, the Manchester United forward lofted the ball

Germany's Lina Magull looks on as defender Millie Bright takes care of business for England

beautifully over her and into the net before celebrating wildly.

The game opened up a little as Germany went in search of an equaliser and they came close as Magull blasted a near-post shot against the frame of the goal, with Earps getting the slightest of touches.

Magull was a constant threat and it was the Bayern Munich star who eventually brought Germany level as sharp work at the near post saw her divert Tabea Wassmuth's low cross past Earps from close range.

Germany finished strongly but extra-time was going to be needed to decide the UEFA Women's EURO final for the first time since 2001.

Tension was ratcheted up a notch as both coaches made use of their subs with the finishing line drawing closer.

A VAR decision on a potential handball in the England penalty area was the biggest drama of the first half of extra-time, but just as the thought of a dreaded penalty shoot-out was starting to enter the heads of players and fans, a winner arrived – and it was another England substitute that did the trick.

Lauren Hemp swung in a corner that bounced goalwards off the body of Lucy Bronze. Chloe Kelly, who had replaced the injured Beth Mead, swivelled and failed to connect well enough with her first effort, but made no mistake with the second, stabbing past Frohms. Kelly ran off, twirling her shirt above her head.

Despite there being so much at stake, England saw out the final 10 minutes with no real alarm bells but when the final whistle went the mixture of relief and joy was obvious.

Some players ran deliriously in random directions, some sat, drained and emotional, on the Wembley turf.

Wiegman, who had won the competition with the Netherlands in 2017, had led England to their first major trophy – and doing it on home soil just made the celebrations all the sweeter.

Ella Toone celebrates her goal after (above) Germany had come closest to scoring in the first half following a goalmouth scramble

Germany goalkeeper Merle Frohms commanded her area well so it took a spectacular effort from Ella Toone (left) to break the deadlock

Chloe Kelly stabs the ball past Merle Frohms at the second attempt – a scruffy goal but it meant so much

Chloe Kelly's celebration will live long in the memory. After a moment of hesitation to check that the goal had been allowed, she ran off towards the England bench twirling her shirt in the air

With medals around their necks, the England players could bask in the glory of being champions

We Play Strong
FOUNDATION
14

England 2 Germany 1 (aet)

Toone 62 Magull 79
Kelly 110

England: Earps, Bronze, Bright, Williamson (c), Daly (Greenwood 88), Stanway (Scott 89), Walsh, Kirby (Toone 56), Mead (Kelly 64), Hemp (Parris 119), White (Russo 56).

Germany: Frohms, Rauch (Lattwein 113), Hegering (Doorsoun 103), Hendrich, Gwinn, Däbritz (Lohmann 73), Oberdorf, Magull (Dallmann 90), Brand (Wassmuth 46), Schüller (Anyomi 67), Huth (c).

UEFA Player of the Match: Keira Walsh

Beth Mead was named Player of the Tournament and finished as top goalscorer

POST-MATCH:

"What we've done is incredible. I knew we had England behind us — we saw that coming to the stadium. But the whole tournament we've had so much support from our fans. I'm so proud of the team. The team has done so well. And without good players you will never win the tournament. But the staff – we have a very big staff and the way they facilitated the team is also very necessary to get the team in the best place possible."

– Sarina Wiegman

UEFA
women's
EURO
ENGLAND 2022
Together
#WePlayStrong
ENGLAND

POST-MATCH:

"Today was not comfortable at all. It was hot, it was humid, it was a very tiring game. You saw how good Germany were and how tough a game it was: two heavyweights going up against each other. I'll never forget these moments. The emotion at full-time was overwhelming, incredible. I'm just so happy that gold is the colour."

– Mary Earps

"What more could you ask for as a player? Playing a home EURO in front of your nation, selling out Wembley – the heart of football in England. The fans have been so incredible. We wanted to remain in our own bubble and we've been really strong with that. But now it's time to embrace being outside of that bubble and connect with our fans on another level. I've heard that the country's gone wild."

– Millie Bright

"It's so special to share this moment with such an amazing bunch of girls. I'm proud to wear this badge, but I'm even more proud to share the pitch with such an unbelievable group of players and unbelievable set of staff."

– Chloe Kelly

BEING CHAMPIONS

In the glowing aftermath of the glory at Wembley, Sarina Wiegman and some of her players tried to take in what they had achieved...

"We won the cup, and it is just unbelievable. If you really want to win, really want to become better every single day, you can do it and that is what I have noticed the whole year.

"We agreed on a couple of things about behaviour and they weren't just words, we lived it and this is the result.

"It's just incredible, they want to do it together.

"Over the whole tournament we've had so much support from our fans. I'm so proud of the whole team. I think I'll need a few days to realise what we've done.

"The quality of this team is so high, and the depth too. When I took the job I knew there was quality in the team and there was such big potential in the country because the development of the game here is really far and there was lots of competition because of how many good players there are so you hope that things will work out.

"My challenge was to bring people together – first staff, then players with the support of The FA – and how it has worked out this year is just incredible. It's what you hope for and it's really nice that it worked out this way."

– Sarina Wiegman

"You talk about things like this so much and for it to actually happen... First of all you've got to be in the final. We took care of that and then to deal with what we've dealt with and enjoy it. I enjoyed it so much!

"But the relief just came because I felt I'd done it the way I wanted to do it and I took in every single moment. I never put too much pressure on myself and as a team we've just re-written the history books.

"I'm just super proud to be English and I think when I play, I play for the badge and this is my way of representing my country and I think that is my greatest asset I suppose.

"And going on this journey with the girls, I'm a leader from within. I don't want to be at the front, I don't want to be anything other than what I've always been but this felt special because all of us have just played our little part along the way. All those tiny little cogs in the wheel and we've just done what we wanted to do.

"I'm proud of myself, of course I'm proud of myself, but I'm proud of the team and so proud to be English."

– Leah Williamson

"I'm going to frame my boots, my shirt and my sports bra probably – absolutely everything!

"It's amazing. This is what dreams are made of and to share the pitch with such a wonderful set of girls, honestly, this is amazing.

"You don't see the background work and each and every part of it, the staff, the players, everyone involved in women's football, this is what it's all about.

"It's unbelievable and I can't put it into words. You dream of these moments as a little girl but to be here at Wembley with 87,500 fans, this is unbelievable.

"Germany were a brilliant team, which makes the final even better, when you have to work so hard for it, these moments feel even better because they were a great team. It was the two best teams in the final.

"We knew at the start of the tournament it was about the wider group, not just the 11 on the pitch and I think that really showed today in our celebrations because we're one team and these great things can happen when you all stick together."

– Chloe Kelly

"I can't believe it. It's such a privilege to be part of this — all the fans, what a day. The younger players have been absolutely fantastic, playing with freedom. You see them come on, they love the game. I don't think I'm going to sleep this week."

– Jill Scott

"It's amazing; something I've dreamed of for a long, long time. To win this now is amazing. It's incredible. To get to the final and get the win is what this team is all about."

– Fran Kirby

"I was a nervous wreck the whole time [after being substituted]. When you're on the pitch you don't feel it and then when you come off, you feel every single emotion."

– Rachel Daly

"I can't believe it. Sometimes football cuts you down, but bouncing back is the best thing to do. I'm still in shock, I can't believe we've won it. I am so proud of this team.

"We're ready to party and celebrate these moments. Sarina Wiegman was so calm. She believed in us, we believed in each other as a team, so she didn't have to say that much but here we are.

"There's been plenty of buzz around but we've been really good at keeping ourselves in our bubble and credit to Sarina and the staff for creating that environment. Today we just aimed to go out and play another game of football so we weren't putting too much pressure on ourselves.

"We're in shock. It hasn't sunk in yet."

– Beth Mead

"It's almost like it was written in the stars for us. Chloe deserves this moment after the hard work she's put in. I'm not sure about taking her top off but she's an unbelievable person. She was in the right place at the right moment and she scored the winning goal so she's a hero.

"We've just won the European final and it's incredible to be doing it with people I've grown up with. It's an unbelievable feeling and it hasn't sunk in yet. The partying is going to last for a few days.

"It's been a real team effort and I'm glad we can all share the trophy.

"In the tough moments the crowd definitely got us through. When we were younger we definitely didn't think we'd be playing in front of 87,000 people – that's where all the tears came from after the game. We hope we've inspired lots of young girls to play football."

– Keira Walsh

"It was an unbelievable 24 hours – everyone was dancing, beers flying everywhere, there's Abba, Céline Dion...

"Players and staff were on the bus; the whole way back to the hotel there was partying. Everyone was everywhere on tables, chairs, down the alleyways.

"It's crazy – now we've seen what the whole outside world has been saying, it's crazy. We're not in our own little bubble anymore, we're off on our own paths now and I'm just over the moon.

"Of course, we always want more. We wanted this, and we've been waiting a long, long time for this and now we've got it, and we want more."

– Ella Toone

"I have not been to any tournaments before so I don't know what it was like previously but to me, that felt like the most together team. Obviously from my point of view of not getting too many minutes, the work ethic that the girls [who didn't start the games] have put in day in and day out has been phenomenal.

"We all came together and did the absolute best that we could.

"For me, I just hope that people all over the world see this and encourage young kids to get involved, play football and follow their dream."

– Jess Carter

"I saw Serena [Wiegman[, I jumped on the table, and then I looked up and saw all the cameras and iPhones and thought, 'oh, God' ... But I committed. I carried on and I wiggled my hips. I got down and I said to Serena 'we're done now', and bolted as fast as possible.

"I don't think it has sunk in yet. I keep feeling like, 'Is this real? Has this happened?'"

– Mary Earps

"The fact the team is in the position that it's in is down to players who came before us like Fara Williams, Steph Houghton, Faye White and the players from the last final. The work they put in means we could start at a high level. We're very fortunate in that respect."

– Lucy Bronze

“We just keep looking at each other and going, ‘Is this fake, has this just actually happened?’ We’re just going to enjoy the moment.
“We’re just buzzing. We’re going to go mad. We’ve won the EUROs so we’re just going to live it up.”

– Georgia Stanway

"It was a rollercoaster. Scoring the first goal, then them scoring so late – that was when the team came together. We've proved before that we can go the distance and we've proved it again today. Unbelievable.

"Chloe's celebration doesn't surprise us one bit. She's full of character, full of life. After the year she's had, what a moment for her."

– Alex Greenwood

"It's been amazing, my first major tournament. The girls were saying it's not always like this.

"The group we've had in this camp has been unbelievable. The talent has always been in England, the calibre of players has always been high and the players who came before us have paved the way for us to win this trophy.

"Everything about this team was special. The players, the staff, the support we were given really set us up for success."

– Alessia Russo

MAKING THE DREAM A REALITY

The perfect legacy: winning the trophy and inspiring the next generation

BY CHRIS BRERETON

The evolution and development of most sports is something that, by definition, usually happens slowly.

The norm is for an inch to be gained here or there, improvements are so gradual that they're barely really acknowledged, and recognition and reward take a while to filter down to all levels.

Yes, just occasionally, the opposite is true.

Some sports do not take small steps, they take giant leaps.

And that can be said of women's football in England. Indeed, we can actually pinpoint the exact moment women's football truly went stratospheric across the nation.

It was 7.32pm on 31 July, 2022, when Ukrainian Kateryna Monzul blew the final whistle on England's sensational 2-1 victory over Germany in the final of UEFA Women's EURO 2022.

Of course, the ongoing increase and involvement in women's football over the past 20 years has already been a marvel to behold and the advent of the Women's Super League, along with hugely increased attendance figures and media involvement, has already brought the sport to the attention of millions.

WINNERS
31 JULY 2022

But the legacy of England's win at EURO 2022 is something else altogether.

The sport is now in overdrive.

When Chloe Kelly poked home against Germany to give England a 2-1 advantage, she did not just make the Lionesses' dreams come true, she paved the way for millions more football-obsessed girls to also follow their own ambitions, as brilliantly pointed out by England legend Ellen White.

White, who retired in August after one of the greatest of all England careers, believes that the win creates a blueprint that can change the face of English sport forever.

She said: "This is for the next generation and potentially the next Lioness: you don't have to be the best at something to make your dreams come true, just look at me. Hard work, dedication, passion and love for what you do are a great recipe.

"Don't ever let someone tell you you can't do something or achieve your dreams. I was once told I couldn't play in the boys' team and I would never play for England. Now I am retiring having made 113 caps with 52 goals for England and a European champion. Go out there and be the very best version of you!

"Let's use the momentum from the EUROs win to make sure that every young person in all communities has the opportunity to play and feel connected to all England football teams."

For a sport to inspire the next generation, it has to be seen and be visible to them and there is no doubt that UEFA Women's EURO 2022 was an astonishing success that saw records tumble in all directions as Europe and the rest of the world truly embraced a fascinating and entertaining tournament.

The final was witnessed live by 87,192 people – a record number of supporters for a EURO game – while across the tournament as a whole, 574,875 fans came through the turnstiles, smashing all previous records by a comfortable margin.

The tournament was the most watched Women's EURO ever as over 365 million

viewers tuned in across TV and streaming channels. That was more than double the number of live viewers compared to the 2017 edition (178 million) and 214 percent more live viewers than in 2013 (116 million).

England's glorious victory in the final was viewed by more than 50 million people worldwide, over three times more than for the 2017 final, and that all points to a hugely positive future for the women's game.

In England, across those huge viewing figures there will be young girls who will have now been inspired to lace up some boots and kick a football about.

If they can see it, they can be it. And there is little doubt that the visibility of UEFA Women's EURO 2022 will play a massive role in encouraging youngsters to take up the game.

Chelsea and England defender Jess Carter said: "For us, we want to inspire the next generation. We want to inspire everybody but to be able to have little kids look up to us and say 'I want to be them' and 'I can be them' is really special.

"For me, I just hope that people all over the world see this and encourage young kids to get involved, play football and follow their dream."

Jess's viewpoint is backed up by her captain Leah Williamson, who agrees that the way UEFA Women's EURO 2022 attracted more viewers to the games can have a lasting impact.

She said: "The legacy of this tournament is the change in society is everything that we've done, we've brought everybody together, we've got people to games. We want

See it, then be it: UEFA Women's EURO 2022 helped viewers to see what can be achieved when you follow your dream

15
UEFA

Inspiring a nation: The new European champions wrote to Conservative Party leadership candidates (right) to urge them to build on the legacy of EURO 2022

them to come to the WSL (Barclays WSL). That is the legacy of this team and that is the start of the journey.

"There will be so many people filling that stadium with an interest in women's football who have an opportunity to watch it because it has been made available, because not so long ago that wasn't the case and I think that is probably one of the nicest things to reflect on."

The players' passion to seize the moment was illustrated by an open letter they wrote to Conservative Party leadership hopefuls Liz Truss and Rishi Sunak immediately after EURO 2022 victory, urging them to back further steps to improve access to football for girls.

A crucial pillar of ensuring the legacy of UEFA Women's EURO 2022 continues long into the future is the hard work and vision of The FA, which worked exceptionally hard prior to the tournament to make footballing opportunities more accessible to young women across the country.

A huge range of initiatives were launched to harness the power of the tournament and

Dear Rishi Sunak and Liz Truss,

On Sunday evening history was made. The dreams of 23 women came true. England became European champions for the first time in history.

Throughout the Euros, we as a team spoke about our legacy and goal to inspire a nation. Many will think that this has already been achieved, but **we see this as only the beginning**. We are looking to the future. We want to create real change in this country and we are asking you, if you were to become Prime Minister on 5 September, to help us achieve that change.

We want every young girl in the nation to be able to play football at school.

Currently only 63% of schools offer football equally to girls and boys in PE lessons. The reality is we are inspiring young girls to play football, only for many to end up going to school and not being able to play.

This is something that we all experienced growing up. We were often stopped from playing. So we made our own teams, we travelled across the country and despite the odds, we just kept playing football.

Women's football has come a long way. But it still has a long way to go.

We ask you and your government to ensure that all girls have access to a minimum of 2hrs a week PE. Not only should we be offering football to all girls, we also need to invest in and support female PE teachers too. Their role is crucial and we need to give them the resources to provide girls' football sessions. They are key role models from which so many young girls can flourish.

We have made incredible strides in the women's game, but this generation of school girls deserve more. They deserve to play football at lunchtime, they deserve to play football in PE lessons and they deserve to believe they can one day play for England. We want their dreams to also come true.

This is an opportunity to make a huge difference. A change that will impact millions of young girls' lives. We – the 23 members of the England Senior Women's EURO squad – ask you to make it a priority to invest into girls' football in schools, so that every girl has the choice.

Regards,

The 2022 UEFA Women's EURO England Squad

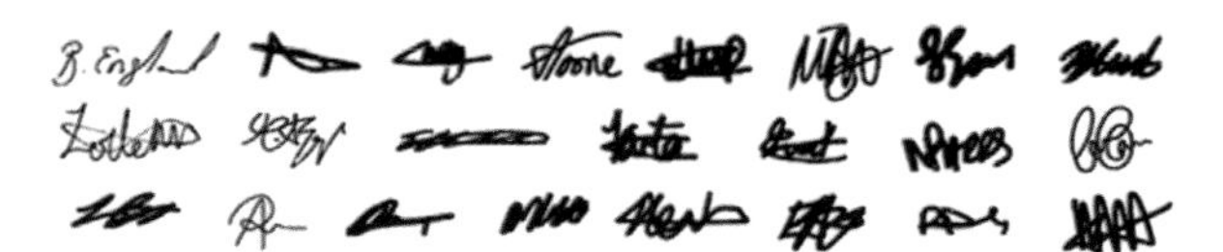

Getting involved: Increased access to football for women and girls is one of the fundamental aims of The FA

again outline to people from all backgrounds that football is for them. In the nine host areas across England – Sheffield, Rotherham, Manchester, Trafford, Wigan & Leigh, Milton Keynes, London, Southampton and Brighton & Hove – legacy plans were put in place which moved all female football opportunities under one umbrella for the first time and which made explicitly clear what The FA's ambitions are across participation, coaching and refereeing up until 2024.

The goal, numbers and scope, of that ambition are truly impressive with three very simple, fundamental goals:

- Equal access for all girls to play football in school and clubs
- Diverse workforce of coaches, referees and local leaders delivering and organising football for their communities
- Inclusive, safe and welcoming environments for every woman and girl to play competitive or recreational grassroots football, irrespective of ability, disability, age or ambition

That clear pathway is also determined to see more than half a million new football opportunities for women and girls with the ultimate goal of seeing 120,000 more girls regularly playing football in schools and clubs, 300 new FA-qualified female coaches, 1,000 women and girls completing the entry-level FA Playmaker Award, 350 new FA-qualified female referees, 20,000 more women playing football for fun, fitness and friendship and 7,000 more women and girls regularly playing competitive football in grassroots clubs.

Fan Festivals lasting the length of the tournament were also set up and were designed to be welcoming, inclusive and encouraging for football fans of all ages.

Those events, and that vision, point to a vital truth about UEFA Women's EURO 2022, and that truth is that as glorious as England's ultimate victory was, it is the longer lasting impact of the tournament that will one day also be spoken of in awe.

And, as has been so often the case since she became the England coach in September 2021, nobody puts it better than Sarina Wiegman.

The mastermind of England's victory has spoken at length about what EURO glory means to her personally but she is also conscious of its wider impact, its wider effect, its wider magic.

"This tournament has done so much for the game but also for women in society," she said. "I don't think

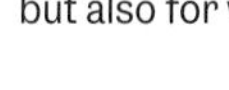

Firing enthusiasm: Whether in a stadium, in a park or at the victory celebrations, the engagement of fans in women's football has hugely increased

UEFA
women's
EURO
ENGLAND 2022

we've really realised what we've done. Over the whole tournament we've had so much support from our fans. We did an incredible job and I'm so proud of my team.

"During our journey to the EURO we brought in players who played in 1971. They were trailblazers for the next generation. We should always remember those who went before us as they made a path for us, and now our players make a path for the next generations.

"I hope that EURO 2022 will lead to many girls starting to play football, but I also hope that women see role models and want to become a football coach or take on a role related to football. So, I'd like to see more female footballers and also more women within football in other roles.

"The FA did everything we needed to be as good as we could be. I'd like to thank everyone who made this tournament so exceptional and took it to the next level. And most of all, we changed society."

You sure did Sarina, you sure did.

England's coach is rightly proud of her team. Indeed, we're all proud of her team, and we're all excited by what the future holds; a future that began in England in 2022.

And a future that has never looked more exciting.

Eye on the future: The young girls of today could be the players, coaches or European champions of tomorrow

UEFA
PHOTO
UEFA
PHOTO
219
UEFA
PHOTO
152
UEFA
PHOTO

ENGLAND PARTNERS
NATIONAL GALLERY
NATIONAL GALLERY

INSPIRING WORDS

"That's what we set out to do in this tournament, make the nation proud, fight for women and get young girls involved as well and I think we've done that for every single woman in this world."

– Ella Toone

"I think it's unbelievable, the way women's football has grown, especially over the last few weeks. Having packed-out stadiums, it's just incredible and to go out on that pitch and hear the crowd roar and then again every single time we score, it just gives us such a boost."

– Lauren Hemp

"I think the state of the game compared to the 2017 EUROs has changed massively.

"For this tournament, there had been something like 450,000 tickets sold [before it started] in comparison to 240,000-odd who attended the EUROs in the Netherlands. It's more than doubled and I think the women's game has more than doubled since then, in such a short space of time.

"It's an exciting prospect to see how well we can do and obviously what it can do for the game in England, as well as the game in general all over the world.

"It's exciting to see how far it can rise and go in the right direction. I think this is the summer where we can do that, where the women's game can get to the next level."

– Beth Mead

STATS

The numbers and facts that matter

ENGLAND AT UEFA WOMEN'S EURO 2022

Goals scored:

22

Goals conceded:

2

Saves:

13

Clean sheets:

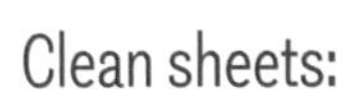

4